Beriah André Watson

**The Sportsman's Paradise; or, the Lake Lands of Canada**

Beriah André Watson

**The Sportsman's Paradise; or, the Lake Lands of Canada**

ISBN/EAN: 9783337186326

Printed in Europe, USA, Canada, Australia, Japan

Cover: Foto ©Andreas Hilbeck / pixelio.de

More available books at **www.hansebooks.com**

# THE SPORTSMAN'S PARADISE;

## OR,

## THE LAKE LANDS OF CANADA.

BY

B. A. WATSON, A.M., M.D.

*WITH ILLUSTRATIONS BY*
DANIEL C. AND HARRY BEARD.

PHILADELPHIA
J. B. LIPPINCOTT COMPANY.
1888.

AFFECTIONATELY INSCRIBED

TO

REV. THOMAS M. KILLEEN,

A STEADFAST FRIEND, AN AGREEABLE COMPANION,
AND A TRUE SPORTSMAN,

BY THE AUTHOR.

# PREFACE.

The acme of pleasure can only be attained by the sportsman when his *confrères* are permitted to share with him in the excitement of the chase. In this respect the chase may be compared to a good dinner, which is always most enjoyable when partaken of in the company of congenial spirits. A book may likewise be further compared to a dinner, since the first chapter is commonly introductory to the better parts which come in the regular order of the courses, while a narrative which produces no pleasurable excitement for the reader is like a dinner without wine.

This *menu* has been prepared for the general reading public, but it is thought by the author that it may be especially enjoyed by sportsmen and the rising generation of boys, who frequently find more pleasure in the perusal of books truthfully delineating the excitement of the chase than in reading those of fiction.

The author is deeply indebted to the accomplished artist, Dan. C. Beard, of New York, who has so greatly assisted him in the presentation of the more interesting parts of this narrative, and also to the publishers, J. B. Lippincott Company, of Philadelphia, whose work speaks so well for the printing art in America.

B. A. WATSON.

Jersey City, N. J., October 12, 1887.

# CONTENTS.

## CHAPTER I.

RECREATION AND ITS OBJECTS—CLASSIFICATION OF HUNTERS—ACTIVE EXERCISE AN EXCELLENT REMEDY FOR OBESITY—SPORT AT SHELBYVILLE, TENNESSEE—WHAT OCCURRED AT THE EVANS HOUSE—A FRIEND IN NEED IS A FRIEND INDEED—HOME ONCE MORE . . . . . . . . 1

## CHAPTER II.

THREE DOCTORS IN SEARCH OF SPORT—OUR GUIDES—THE CHIEF, AND THE MAGNET WHICH CONTROLLED HIM—TROUT-FISHING ON SUNDAY, AND THE RESULTS WHICH FOLLOWED A VIOLATION OF THE CANADIAN LAW—CHIEF JOHN IN DISGRACE—FAILURE OF HIS PLANS . . . . . . . 20

## CHAPTER III.

GRAND FISHING EXCURSION—WATTE'S CREEK VISITED BY THE GOVERNOR AND ESCULAPIUS—THEIR RETURN AND RECEPTION AT CAMP—GRAND DEER-HUNT, LED BY DR. POKORNEY—CHIEF JOHN AND HIS ASSISTANTS ARE RELIEVED FROM DUTY AND GO TO THE REAR IN DISGRACE—DR. POKORNEY AND OTHER ASSISTANTS . . . . . . . . . 41

## CHAPTER IV.

THE START AND INCIDENTS OF THE JOURNEY—LUMBERMEN AND THEIR DRUNKEN ORGIES—TRAVELLING BY THE ROYAL MAIL STAGE IN MUSKOKA—THE PARTY ATTACKED BY FLEAS—CAMP ON CANOE LAKE—DEER-HUNTING—GOVERNOR STARTS FOR HOME—THE REMAINDER OF THE PARTY OFF FOR NEW FIELDS—CAMP ON PICKEREL LAKE—RAIN AND FISH—CROSSING THE HORKA-PORKA PORTAGE—CAMP ON ROCK LAKE—TROUT-FISHING—CAMP NEAR LOON AND GRASS LAKES—CAMP ON SAND LAKE—HOMEWARD BOUND . . . . . . . . . . 61

## CONTENTS.

### CHAPTER V.

THE START FOR A GRAND MOOSE- AND DEER-HUNT—SELECTION OF A PHOTOGRAPHER AND THE CHIEF GUIDE—A ROMANTIC WEDDING AND THE HONEYMOON—ARRIVAL AT ROSSEAU VILLAGE—CANADIAN STAGE ROUTE—PROPRIETOR AND DRIVER—OUR OLD FRIEND "CHRIS"—OUR NEW-MADE ACQUAINTANCE—MR. STRUCE, OF BROOKLYN . . . . . . 80

### CHAPTER VI.

OUR DEPARTURE FROM ROSSEAU—A CHARMING MORNING AND A HEALTHFUL WALK—CAMPED NEAR SPENCE—INCIDENTS WHICH OCCURRED THERE—JOINED BY OUR GUIDES—CAMPED ON BIRCH ISLAND—CAMP-LIFE ON AHMIC LAKE—STRUCE STARTS FOR HOME—THE BALANCE OF THE PARTY OFF ON A LONG TRAMP—THE BEAVER'S TRYSTING-PLACES—THE PHOTOGRAPHER'S SPORT NEAR BURK'S FALLS—PLODDING THROUGH WOODS AFTER DARK—THE YOUTHFUL DRIVER—ARRIVAL AT SPHYNX SHOOT . . . . 102

### CHAPTER VII.

THE MOVEMENTS OF OUR HUNTING-PARTY—CROSSING THE HOR-KA-POR-KA PORTAGE—FISHING IN ROCK LAKE—ANOTHER ADVANCE—DEER-HUNTING, ETC.—THE JOURNEY FROM TROUT LAKE TO LONG LAKE—CAMP ON LONG LAKE—MORE DEER-HUNTING—AN EXCITING CONTEST, IN WHICH THE PHOTOGRAPHER WINS . . . . . . . . . . . 124

### CHAPTER VIII.

DRYING VENISON—A GRAND AND BEAUTIFUL MOUNTAIN GORGE—THE MEETING AT THE BEAVER-DAM—OUR PHOTOGRAPHER LOST IN THE WILDERNESS—A LONELY NIGHT ON BUCK LAKE—THE HORRIBLE DREAM—THE LOST MAN FOUND—THE UNEXPECTED MEETING WITH A BULL MOOSE . . 146

### CHAPTER IX.

A SHOT AT A BULL MOOSE—FOLLOWING THE MOOSE-TRAIL—MOOSE-CALLING—BREAKING CAMP ON LONG LAKE—CAMP ON TRAIL BETWEEN UPPER LONG AND SUGAR-BUSH LAKES—BAD WEATHER AND CONSEQUENT DELAY—PREPARATION AND START ON THE RECONNOISSANCE . . . . 167

## CHAPTER X.

THE FIRST DINNER—KILLED A DEER—FOLLOWING A MOOSE-TRAIL—CAMPED ON THE TRAIL—PREPARATION FOR SPENDING THE NIGHT—OUR LEAN-TO—A SNOW-STORM—LONG, DREARY TRAMP—DISCOVERY OF A MOOSE-YARD—A HIGHLY-EXCITING CHASE—KILLED TWO RED DEER—A DISGUSTED AND ANGRY CAPTAIN—HONEST TOIL BRINGS REFRESHING SLEEP—THE HUNT RESUMED . . . . . . . . . . 189

## CHAPTER XI.

THE DISCOVERY OF MOOSE—THE KILLING OF TWO MOOSE AND THE WOUNDING OF ANOTHER—OUR CAMP ON MOOSE HILL—THE RETURN TO SUGAR-BUSH LAKE—A SEVERE RAIN-STORM—RETURN TO MOOSE HILL—THE DEAD MOOSE PHOTOGRAPHED—ANOTHER EXPEDITION—THE BEAR—A SNOW-STORM—A HARD TRAMP . . . . . . . 210

## CHAPTER XII.

THE BEAR WHICH WAS NOT KILLED—FOLLOWING THE MOOSE—THE CAPTAIN KILLED THE BULL MOOSE—PACKING OUT OF THE WOODS—THE REST AT HARKNESS'S SHACK—A HARD TRAMP—BURK'S FALLS—A DEER-HUNT—ANOTHER TRIP TO CANADA IN THE COMPANY OF MY SON, A LAD OF FIFTEEN—TEACHING THE BOY TO SHOOT—KILLED HIS FIRST DEER—AN EXCITING CHASE—THE OLD DOE MAKES HER ESCAPE . . . 235

## CHAPTER XIII.

THE CONTINUANCE OF THE DEER-HUNT—AN EXCITING CHASE—BRILLIANT MANŒUVRING OF AN OLD BUCK—BREAKING CAMP ON THE ISLAND—A PARTRIDGE-HUNT BY THE ROADSIDE—AN EXCITING RACE BETWEEN "JIM" AND THE OLD COCKER-SPANIEL—OUR RETURN TO MAGANETAWAN—THE TRIP FROM MAGANETAWAN TO TORONTO . . . . 260

# LIST OF ILLUSTRATIONS.

| | |
|---|---|
| CAMP ON LONG LAKE | *Frontispiece.* |
| "WE IMMEDIATELY WALKED UP TO THE OFFICE, EACH CARRYING A DOUBLE-BARRELLED SHOT-GUN, FOLLOWED BY THREE HUNTING-DOGS" | Page 15 |
| "SAY NOTHING ABOUT THE CONDITION OF OUR CLOTHING" | " 29 |
| SWALLOWING FISH AND FISH-STORIES | " 48 |
| "HE HAS EVADED THE DOG, BUT—" | " 52 |
| "TUESDAY, THE GOVERNOR AND MYSELF EACH SHOT A DEER" | " 67 |
| "IT IS A SERIOUS THING TO GET LOST IN THE WILDS OF CANADA" | " 76 |
| A WEDDING IN THE WILDERNESS | " 95 |
| "I DON'T BELIEVE SHE KNOWS THAT SHE IS WANTED" | " 108 |
| WE ARE READY FOR THE JOURNEY | " 129 |
| "HE SHOT THE DEER JUST AS IT BROKE FROM COVER" | " 133 |
| BEAVER-DAM AND HOUSE | " 150 |
| "THE FIRST GLANCE WHICH I OBTAINED OF THIS HUGE ANIMAL WAS WHILE HE WAS STANDING WITH HIS SIDE TOWARDS ME" | " 168 |
| THE WOODS ARE FULL OF THEM | " 201 |
| "FIRE AT HIM!" | " 213 |
| THE DEAD MONARCH | " 217 |
| THE NEAREST SETTLEMENT | " 234 |
| FOOD FOR THE RAVENS LEFT BY BRUIN | " 236 |
| A HARD TRAMP—HOMEWARD BOUND | " 242 |
| "WE FOUND THEM STANDING ON THE DRY GROUND, WHILE THE DOE WAS LYING AT THEIR FEET AND THE HOUNDS WERE FAWNING ABOUT THEM" | " 265 |
| THE DEAD DOE | " 267 |
| THAT RETRIEVER | " 285 |

# THE SPORTSMAN'S PARADISE;

OR, THE

# LAKE LANDS OF CANADA.

## CHAPTER I.

RECREATION AND ITS OBJECTS—CLASSIFICATION OF HUNTERS—ACTIVE EXERCISE AN EXCELLENT REMEDY FOR OBESITY—SPORT AT SHELBYVILLE, TENN.—WHAT OCCURRED AT THE EVANS HOUSE—A FRIEND IN NEED IS A FRIEND INDEED—HOME ONCE MORE.

THE prudent business man, before making an investment or inaugurating any important change in his affairs, is accustomed to ask the question, Will it pay? Is it a good investment? The same question may be properly asked by any person prior to his departure for the great forests of the Dominion of Canada.

The answer to this query must generally depend on the physical condition of the individual and his appreciation of the sports which are obtainable in these grand forests.

Man, in all conditions of life, after prolonged and earnest toil, requires recreation,—*i.e.*, a refreshment of strength and spirits; but this cannot always be obtainable in the same way. The overwrought workingman, in the full possession of physical energy, in perfect health, and possessed of the ordinary amount of physical strength, does not require the same sort of recreation as the sedentary, overworked student, professional or business man. In the former instance, a few days' rest, with an increased amount of sleep, serves to fully restore the temporarily depressed physical and mental vigor.

The intelligent practice of the fatigued German workingman, who gathers his family about him and hies away to some neighboring grove, where he spends a peaceful and quiet holiday, thus obtaining pure air and rest, cannot be too highly commended. The whole family having spent a pleasant and profitable day in the open air, commonly return to their overcrowded and badly-ventilated apartments in the early evening; each member of the family being better satisfied with himself, and what is still better, satisfied with the others, they now partake of their frugal meal, and retire early to their humble cots, where they may sleep soundly, *suffering neither from insomnia nor frightful dreams*, but awake in the morning completely refreshed. Consequently the Sabbath comes to the workingman as a complete restorer, as a day of perfect recreation.

Physical exertion commonly produces only bodily fatigue, while the vital organs are maintained by the same power in a healthy state, and their various functions are performed in the best possible manner. It is therefore apparent that the physical condition of workingmen is not generally such as to require the active exercise which the hunter gains by the Canadian chase, especially when stalking his game; but a high appreciation of the sport may be an ample compensation for every expenditure.

It may be mentioned in this connection that various hunting-parties seek recreation in the forest in divers ways; and consequently it is necessary to offer on this point an explanation for the benefit of the uninitiated, although no attempt will be made to give a complete classification. The heterogeneous mass of men entering the forest with guns and dogs are generally supposed to be hunters, but in fact among these may be frequently found men whose peculiarities of mind and tastes are more nearly allied to those of Oscar Wilde than to those of Daniel Boone. It is therefore natural that these game-seekers should be continually looking for a hunter's paradise in the shape of a first-class hotel, in the midst of a grand forest, from the porticoes of which can be shot the great moose, the beautiful deer, and all the other species of smaller game, while the same must be accessible by an elegant steamer or grand palace-car.

This class of hunters are continually fault-finding, are never happy, and seem to wish their companions to be as miserable as themselves. They never enter the woods without returning to their homes disgusted and thoroughly dissatisfied. Another class, commonly calling themselves sportsmen, frequently start from their homes heavily laden with kegs, demijohns, and numerous boxes well filled with bottles; and it may here be added that their luggage conveys a correct idea of the recreation which they may be expected to obtain when partially withdrawn from the restrictions imposed upon them by the rules of civilization. It will not be necessary for the accomplishment of their purpose that they should traverse wide tracts of wilderness, or be supplied with the most improved guns, the best dogs, or a large amount of food, since the free imbibition of the spirits with which they are so abundantly supplied will assuredly give them a highly spiritual nature, in which condition they should not be expected to join in the chase or perform any other acts which commonly characterize the ordinary corporeal man. It will therefore be sufficient for their purposes that they withdraw from our crowded thoroughfares to some quiet nook, village, or grove, where, in cabin or tent, surrounded by some congenial guides,—boon companions,—they succeed in whiling away a few days or weeks in a style which has always honored the memory of Tam O'Shanter.

It is not very unusual, even among these parties, when the effects of their deep imbibition have passed away, to find them engaged in target-practice, and they may occasionally sally forth for a few hours in search of game. It is generally a matter of some pride with these so-called sportsmen to be able to say that they shot, during their sojourn in the land of game, one or more deer, and to accomplish this purpose it is said to be not an infrequent practice with them to send out their guides with instructions to purchase one of these desirable animals, which had been previously taken in the chase by some other hunter; the bargain having been made, the deer is brought to the ambitious sportsman, who then fires a charge of buck-shot or a rifle-bullet into the dead carcass, and on this act his claim to have shot or killed the much-coveted game is based.

Having now mentioned some of the characteristics of the pseudo-sportsman, we turn, with increased pleasure, to a consideration of the more noble character,—the true hunter. The true hunter, in many particulars, resembles the true soldier, and in several respects their lives are essentially the same: both are inured to hardships and likewise exposed to dangers, while unusual fatigue, severe and often prolonged deprivation, are their common lot. Both are stimulated by conquest and likewise depressed by failure. The true hunter's enthusiasm, like the true soldier's, resembles, in some respects, the spirit which animates, under certain circumstances, the old war-horse and the decrepit hunting-dog. Instances are occasionally related in which a noble charger has been compelled by adverse circumstances to accept service on the farm in his old age; but even now, when harnessed to the plough, we are told that this noble animal is frequently so excited by the bugle-notes sounding the cavalry charge that he rears his head and tail, cocks his ears, and dashes away in search of an unseen enemy,—showing that he has not yet lost his fires of youth, and that he still desires to participate in the bloody work of war,—to hear the boom of the cannon, the rattling shots of the carbine, or to see the flashes of the glittering sabres. The old, decrepit hunting-dog, half blinded by age, stiffened in every limb by rheumatism, having been compelled by infirmities to remain in the kitchen corner for years, is aroused to a new life by the click of a gun-lock, raises his eyes towards his master's face, staggers to his feet, and once more expresses his love of the chase by jumping about the hunter's limbs, lovingly caressing his hands, and following on with the other dogs, hunting through field and forest until his strength completely fails, then uttering a dismal howl,—proclaiming his disappointment and rage caused by his inability to go farther,—falls to the ground and frequently fails to reach again the kitchen corner, but is often mercifully relieved from further suffering by death in this last effort. The true sportsman is possessed of a high degree of enthusiasm,— he joins in the chase because it gives him pleasure,—excitement which it produces causes him to forget, for the time, hunger and fatigue. He therefore follows the game from morning until night. His food is commonly plain, but nutritious, still no one enjoys eating more than the sportsman, since his system has been fully prepared for the food, and it may be further added that the food is adapted for the wants of the body. The hunter makes his bed on smooth mother-earth, spreads his rubber blanket over the sweet-scented balsam branches, or should his time be too much occupied with other matters, then these branches will be omitted, but without seriously interfering with his repose.

It is important to remember in this connection that those who have lived a sedentary and studious life are particularly prone to suffer from various forms of dyspepsia and likewise insomnia. *It may also be boldly asserted at this point, without entering into any long inquiry bearing on the etiological or pathological conditions of these morbid states, that the man who will engage in the chase with all the enthusiasm of a true sportsman, and will follow the same a few months, will certainly find more benefit from this course of procedure than could possibly be obtained by the most systematic restrictions in the use of food.* Active exercise thus obtained will efficiently relieve obesity and also develop the muscular system.

In this manner it is entirely practical, and at the same time free from danger, to reduce the weight to any desired standard, and that, too, while the diet is wholly unrestrained, except by the exigencies which are inseparable from the life of a hunter in the forest, more or less removed from the luxuries of modern civilization. In this instance a reduction of weight is effected almost entirely by the active and prolonged exercise, which, instead of being a drudgery hard to be borne, is a noble sort of labor which gives rise to the most pleasant thoughts, and at the same time gratifies an exalted ambition.

The literary man who joins in the chase with true sportsmen will very soon discover that hunting is both a science and an art; and consequently this pastime supplies him with the necessary occupation for both body and mind. The *modus operandi* by which it is accomplished is easily comprehended by any thoughtful person. The loss of adipose tissue depends almost entirely, in this case, on the exercise taken, while the increased muscular development is due to the same agency. It will therefore be observed that depriving fat patients of certain sorts of food which are frequently considered by them as essential to their happiness is not required by this method of treatment.

The athlete generally depends for the reduction of weight on this system of active exercise rather than on any restrictions of diet. Furthermore, there is no doubt that if this simple method of treating obesity was fully understood it would be very popular with those affected with a tendency to an over-accumulation of fat, since personal deformity would thus be avoided, and the individual so relieved would be enabled to perform his rôle in life as a worker and bread-winner with increased ease.

The science of cookery has now attained to such a degree of perfection as to promote epicurean tastes, and likewise to lead to extensive gormandizing, especially among the rich and those of sedentary habits. Its evil effects become most apparent in middle life, while it cannot be denied that in many instances it is carried forward into old age. During childhood and early life, the age of great physical activity, obesity is rarely seen. This fact speaks volumes in favor of active physical exercise as an agency for the prevention of obesity; but it is not to be supposed that every person overburdened with fat will possess the required energy to exercise sufficiently to materially diminish this undesirable burden. Many of them will be seen waddling about our cities, even when the temperature is below seventy degrees Fahrenheit, puffing and blowing like a wind-broken horse while being exercised, and when the weather becomes warmer these unfortunate mortals are compelled to employ fans, seek rest in shady nooks, imbibe ice-water and other cooling drinks in order to relieve, so far as possible, their present misery.

The efforts made by these very corpulent persons to secure merely present relief forcibly remind me of the action of an over-fattened hog on a hot July day, when it half buries itself in the cool earth, mud, or any other cooling substance which may be accessible to the poor sufferer, and in which it commonly remains, uttering only an occasional grunt, until food is again placed before it, when it once more gorges itself. So lives our typical fat man. So lives our over-fattened hog. Both live only to eat, but do not eat to live. Let it be ever remembered that physical activity is antagonistic to an excessive accumulation of fat in the whole animal creation, and, consequently, the ever-active weasel, fox, and many other active animals which might be mentioned are never burdened with obesity.

It may be boldly asserted that physical activity is the very best prophylactic agent which has ever been employed against obesity, and that it is also entitled to a high rank as a curative means in the treatment of the same morbid condition. It must be evident to every thinking person that the time spent by our overworked sedentary students, professional and business men at Long Branch, Newport, Saratoga, and other fashionable resorts does not yield them ample returns: it does not supply them with complete recreation, but only idleness,—a condition of things better calculated to do good to the overworked farmer and mechanic. This remark is likewise applicable to the majority of the middle-aged ladies who are found lounging away their time in these places, while the younger ladies, who dance, ride on horseback, and otherwise exercise, cannot be placed in the same category.

There are certain conditions which are absolutely necessary to a high degree of bodily health, and among them may be mentioned, as being of the highest importance, physical exercise, pure air, the proper quantity of wholesome food, and sufficient sleep.

Having given our attention to the subject of obesity, we will now turn to the consideration of some of the affections connected with the alimentary canal and nervous system. These diseases are specially common among sedentary persons and those engaged in literary pursuits; therefore professional and business men are frequently their victims. I am able to call to mind the case of a lawyer who has always been very irregular in regard to the quality and quantity of food which he has taken since he commenced the practice of his profession, and, as might naturally be anticipated, inasmuch as he has entirely disregarded all the well-known laws of digestion for about fifteen years, he is now paying the penalty which is required of those who violate these natural regulations, since he suffers severely from dyspepsia. However, it should not be inferred that his disregard of the natural laws has been fully and specifically expressed in the above statement, since, in addition to what has already been said, it should have been added that he has generally regulated his hours for sleep by the amount of time which he has been able to spare from study and other mental efforts; and inasmuch as he has never been able to keep up with these demands, his hours for repose have been generally insufficient and very irregular.

Let us now enter more specifically into a consideration of his irregularities of diet, and it may be here assumed, for the purpose of illustrating our subject, that this busy man has been accustomed to rise at six o'clock in the morning, breakfast hurriedly on a cold potato, rush off to business, keep himself at the boiling heat of excitement until one P.M., when he may enter some eating-house, swallow quickly some sauer-kraut and ice-cream, going through about the same business performance in the afternoon as in the morning, maintaining about the same temperature; but when six o'clock P.M. is reached you may possibly find him sitting down at a well-provided table, bolting, as rapidly as possible, his dinner, that he may be able to spend at least six hours after this meal in studying a case which he is expected to try in court the following day. I have been informed, however, that he occasionally misses a dinner, and that if search be made in his bedroom you will find him there, lamenting his sad fate and complaining loudly of a severe pain in his abdomen. The same gentleman further disregards the rules of health by an intemperate use of tobacco,—chewing as well as smoking,—and frequently entering the dining-room while using the weed, which he only discards in time to begin the mastication of food. Is it strange that this gentleman, having followed such a life for about fifteen years, should now find himself suffering with dyspepsia, insomnia, and hypochondriasis? Is it not strange, on the contrary, that he is still living? The practical question which now presents itself for our consideration is, How can he be benefited? Does he require medicine? *The answer to this question must be emphatically, no! He must have recreation, and having been thus brought into a healthy state, he must then be brought to obey the laws of nature, to live and work like a rational man.*

The unexplored wilderness affords the most inviting field for the required recreation in these cases, and offers, at the same time, the most favorable conditions for the restoration of this class of cases, especially if the patient can be prevailed upon to lead the life of an active, industrious hunter.

In the wilderness the patient is removed from every temptation to any sort of mental labor; he is undisturbed by business or any other outside communications, since he is far from post-office or telegraph. The new order of business, if engaged in stalking game, is tramp, tramp, during the live-long day, while the mind is occupied with pleasant anticipations of prospective or present sport; the blood courses through its vessels with unwonted vigor, the lungs are fully and rapidly inflated with pure air, which very seldom happens among sedentary persons, although so important to the health of all classes; a wholesome appetite is engendered by this active exercise, and after spending a delightful evening around the brightly blazing camp-fire, where a rehearsal of the adventures of the day, with story and song, enliven the hour, the sportsman retires to his couch beneath his canvas tent or lean-to, where his blankets have been spread for him by his guides on balsam boughs which are giving forth their agreeable perfume.

On these he soon falls asleep without rocking or song,—sleeps during the entire night, and awakens in the morning fully refreshed and prepared for another day's toil. Thus passes day after day with the true sportsman in the forest.

Illustrating the health-giving power of active exercise, the author will here briefly refer to a trip which he recently made to Shelbyville, Tennessee, in company with his legal friend whose case has already been mentioned; and here it should be also stated that this lawyer had terminated, on the day of his departure for the South, a series of important trials, and was, therefore, in a highly nervous state. This nervous excitability was very marked in all his movements and doings during our journey. We reached War Trace about three o'clock in the morning, rested until six A.M., when we started out with our guns and dogs for Shelbyville, distant from the former place about eight miles. We had determined to spend the day with the quail, which are very abundant in this part of the State, and to bring up in time for the evening meal at the Evans House in Shelbyville.

It was a warm autumn day, but the excitement of the sport kept us pretty steadily in motion. It was not, therefore, until late in the afternoon when we began to think of food, rest, and shelter; and now, inasmuch as we had made a good bag of birds, it seemed entirely proper to abandon any further search for game and take the direct route for the hotel, which was reached about five o'clock. The moment we left the fields, entered the road, and began to plod along towards our destination, the spirit of the sportsman immediately abandoned us, and then we realized that we were sorely fatigued: every step was painful, the walking was miserable drudgery; we walked a few rods and then halted; started on again; our progress was slow, but we could not remain where we were,—we must go forward. The desired haven was at last reached. We immediately walked up to the office, each carrying a double-barrelled shot-gun, followed by three hunting-dogs, registered our names and that of the gunner who accompanied us, asked for our rooms, to which we were promptly conducted, threw off some portions of our wardrobe which had been burdensome during the greater part of the day, indulged momentarily in a brevet-bath, dropped without further delay on the beds with which our rooms were provided, and within ten minutes each man in the party was sleeping soundly, and continued to sleep for about two hours, when we were called to the evening meal, arose from our beds greatly refreshed, made our toilets, after which we partook of a hearty meal and again returned to our rooms, where we recounted some of the events of the day, then retired in good order to our couches, where we all slept soundly during the entire night, my legal friend forgetting for the time being that he had ever suffered from insomnia or anything else.

We were aroused in the morning by the loud ringing of a bell, which, in this hotel, was used to announce the time for rising and also the proper moment for entering the dining-room for meals. We responded in due time to the demand which had been made upon us by this ringing, and consequently we were prepared to obey the

"We immediately walked up to the office, each carrying a double-barrelled shot-gun, followed by three hunting-dogs."

second summons which informed us that breakfast was now ready. However, owing to greater promptness on the part of others, there were seated around the large hotel table about twenty persons at the time we entered the dining-room, who were observed to cast sidelong glances at us without speaking. Few words were spoken during this meal by any of the guests, but our party was closely eyed. It was not, however, until after breakfast that the lawyer and myself learned the purport of all this when our gunner, Alfred Goldsmith, called my legal friend aside and informed him that the proprietor of the hotel did not seem to be quite at ease in regard to the nature of our business. The lawyer informed me, after his interview with Mr. Goldsmith, that the proprietor had been quizzing our gunner in regard to our intentions in visiting that section of country. When informed by the latter that we came from New York to Tennessee for a few days' quail-shooting, the proprietor expressed, emphatically, his doubts in regard to the accuracy of this statement, and promptly informed Goldsmith that he was not prepared to believe that the gentlemen with him *were such fools as to travel so far merely to kill a few birds.* This remark was too much for Goldsmith; he had no answer for it. The proprietor observing his silence, informed him that he had had the honor of entertaining, within a few months, Jesse James and his party, and that while stopping in this hotel they had occupied the same rooms in which we were now lodged. Goldsmith was now asked if he was familiar with the different points of interest about Shelbyville. He answered in the negative.

The proprietor then mentioned many objects of local interest, among others the hangman's tree, situated about four miles from the hotel, and also added that there had already been hung about a half-dozen persons from its branches. Poor Goldsmith was now thoroughly frightened, and therefore communicated promptly with my legal friend, in order that any threatening misfortune might be avoided. The lawyer and myself having learned that there was really some anxiety manifested in regard to our intentions, promptly determined to call to our assistance John Royall, our former classmate, now living near this hotel, and who was sufficiently acquainted with my legal friend to be able to vouch for his honesty and truthfulness. There was no time lost, inasmuch as we proceeded immediately to the office and asked to be directed to the drug house of John Royall & Co. The hotel clerk gave the required information, and my legal friend promptly departed, determined to have all these suspicions speedily removed, consequently I was not surprised when I was requested, half an hour later, to meet Mr. Royall in the hotel office. An introduction to the proprietor by Mr. Royall was the next business in order.

The hotel proprietor, soon after this introduction by Mr. Royall, took occasion to interview him privately. The result of this interview having proved entirely satisfactory to our host, a new and more pleasant relation with us was immediately inaugurated in the hotel. The proprietor and the guests no longer regarded us with either suspicion or anxiety. The former, however, remarked subsequently to Mr. Royall, with whom he was very well acquainted, that it did, at first, seem very strange that gentlemen would travel so far to shoot a few little birds; and he had thought it much more probable that we were in the employ of the United States government for the purpose of hunting up moonshiners, who at the time were making much trouble in the Southern States.

It may now assist some of my readers if I offer a slight explanation in regard to the cause of the excitement which we had so unintentionally produced. It should be first stated, in this connection, that neither the quail nor any other small birds are often hunted by gentlemen in that vicinity, but it does occasionally happen that some citizen is seen carrying a double-barrelled shot-gun for the purpose of taking the life of a fellow-man, or with the intention of defending himself against those enemies who are supposed to be seeking his blood. An interesting instance of the latter was related to us while sojourning in Shelbyville. Our old classmate and friend not only righted matters for us at the hotel but joined in our field sports, introduced us to his friends, who vied with him in entertaining us, gave us grand dinners, and paid us many other attentions, which seems to be only a part of the true hospitality which pervades the South.

Like the other pleasant parts of our lives, our stay in Shelbyville had its end; and having spent nearly two weeks with our new-made friends, we returned to our homes much improved in health, my legal friend being now able to sleep, while my own diabetic trouble had been much improved.

The question may be properly asked, if we spent our

time in the best possible manner. I am able *to assert positively that our time was spent most agreeably.* The field sports were for us true recreation, but these splendid entertainments must be classed with the milder forms of dissipation.

## CHAPTER II.

THREE DOCTORS IN SEARCH OF SPORT—OUR GUIDES—THE CHIEF, AND THE MAGNET WHICH CONTROLLED HIM—TROUT-FISHING ON SUNDAY, AND THE RESULTS WHICH FOLLOWED A VIOLATION OF THE CANADIAN LAW—CHIEF JOHN IN DISGRACE—FAILURE OF HIS PLANS.

HE author desires to preface this narrative with the statement that nearly nine years have elapsed since these events transpired, and, inasmuch as no notes were taken at the time of the occurrences, it may be necessary for the reader to make some allowance for want of accuracy in some of the minor details.

Furthermore, inasmuch as my companions were exceedingly modest men, who might blush even at the sight of their printed names on these pages, we will designate the leader of our party as Governor, a title which well becomes the aristocratic dignity of this fine old gentleman. A further description of the Governor, as he appeared at the time of which we are now writing, may possess additional interest for our readers; and therefore we will add that, although we have here spoken of him as an old gentleman, it is quite doubtful if he had then attained his sixtieth year. Nevertheless, his hair was already silvered with age, while his step was slow and slightly unsteady; figure erect; height about five feet ten inches; possessed of a rather broad chest, while in other respects his form approximated the aldermanic; complexion light; face full well rounded, partially covered by side-whiskers, and showing at various points enlivening reddish tints caused by a dilation of the capillary blood-vessels; eyes moderately large, and of a grayish color; while neither the nose, mouth, nor chin possessed any marked peculiarities calling for a particular description. His manner of speech was slow and often hesitating, occasionally expressing his wishes and views by silence rather than words. He also maintained a dignified bearing under all circumstances, however trying the situation, and was never known, even in the backwoods, to remove his high choker or spotless linen. He would not even drink tea or coffee from any other vessel than pure china, while a silver spoon, knife, and fork were absolutely essential to his happiness. It must already be apparent to our reader that the Governor possessed, in a very high degree, those important qualifications which so admirably fitted him for the performance of the manifold duties of an ambassador rather than those of a high general or an adventurous leader; consequently I am fully assured that no surprise will be felt when I assert that a further perusal of this chapter will establish the fact that it was in the performance of his ministerial duties that he won his chief laurels.

The other members of this famous hunting-party occupied subordinate positions; consequently no detailed description will be given of them, although we shall hereafter speak of one as Esculapius and the other as Scribe; while the name by which the former is commonly known among his friends might indicate to the uninitiated that his ancestry were originally inhabitants of Finland. It may, however, in this instance, be pardonable to say of Esculapius that his personal appearance, conversation, and movements all declare to the world that he is a sturdy member of the medical profession, possessed of a strong belief of the propriety of enforcing the laws of self-preservation, while the frequency with which he discharged his gun when in the pursuit of game was certainly sufficient to satisfy his companions that he believed gunpowder was made to be burned; but the effect of these shots having never been known, it must always remain an open question whether the game or game-seeker occupied the safer position.

It was early in the month of September when this party took their departure from Jersey City by way of the Erie Railroad, leaving behind them Gotham, with all its wicked, noisome, and enchanting surroundings.

Nothing transpired worthy the attention of the Scribe until we reached the Canadian custom-house on the north side of the Niagara River. Here we met a fine old Irish gentleman,—Canadian custom-house officer,—who examined our baggage, passed and properly marked the same, and then made himself known to us as a brother-sportsman possessing a lively interest in our prospective sports. I cannot with this brief notice pass so lightly by this magnificent specimen of the human family, with whom I had not previously met, although since that meeting I have had several opportunities to listen to his lively stories and enjoy his generous hospitality. I believe he is the son of a distinguished major who at some former time commanded a Canadian fort in the vicinity of the Niagara Falls, having received his commission from the English government. The major's son, the present custom-house officer, stands fully six feet and three inches without boots; is as straight as an arrow, well proportioned, and possessed of a military bearing; while, in addition to all this, he is prompt and courteous in the discharge of his official duties. Having examined our baggage on this occasion, he entered our car, where he remained in conversation with us nearly an hour, until our train was ready to proceed. In this conversation he imparted to us much practical information relating to the selection of guides, the Canadian localities in which we would be most likely to find game, etc. In answer to our inquiry in regard to the habits of the Indian guides, he replied, "They are generally lazy, filthy fellows, less desirable as companions and servants than the native Canadian trappers and backwoodsmen." In support of these views here expressed he gave us a detailed statement of personal observations made while in camp with some friends who had employed Indian guides. The old gentleman spoke particularly of an observation made by himself in the early morning, while the Indian guide was engaged in cleaning the frying-pan preparatory to cooking the breakfast for the hunters. In this instance, the weather being warm, the wardrobe for the body was limited to a single garment, which he now saw the "noble red man" using for the purpose of drying and cleansing the more important cooking utensil. In explanation of the garment,—size, texture, etc.,—he added that it was a common towel which the hunters had brought with them for the purpose of drying the hands of the guides while engaged in cooking, etc., a refinement wholly incomprehensible to the Indian mind, and consequently it had been employed for a very different purpose. He also spoke of their long, unkempt hair, its numerous inhabitants, the effects produced by shaking and brushing it over food and blankets, with much of the same nature. During the narration of these somewhat important events I had watched carefully the deepening expressions on the Governor's face: dark clouds had gathered; I could readily read "No red man need apply;" while even the countenance of Esculapius was no less expressive; but here I read "Death to the dirty dogs; I have no sympathy with them." The Governor's feelings were certainly too deep to find expression in words at this time. He had remained entirely silent during the whole conversation. Esculapius had spoken only a few words, merely in monosyllables; he was apparently overwhelmed with the situation. The old custom-house officer's face was now wreathed in smiles: he had put it forcibly, had watched carefully the effects of the narrative on these amateur sportsmen. As our train was now ready to start, he bade us good-by, wished us success and a pleasant time in Canada, and we were off for the woods.

We proceeded from Niagara Falls immediately to Toronto, remaining overnight at the Queen's Hotel. In the mean time the Governor telegraphed to various persons in different parts of the province of Ontario for guides, etc. Replies having been received, it was determined to start for Bracebridge some time during the following day, where we would meet guides who had already been selected for us through the efforts of the Governor.

In accordance with this decision we left Toronto in the afternoon, travelled by rail as far as the Muskoka wharf, which is situated on Lake Muskoka, and from this point by a small steamer, which reached Bracebridge about midnight. The instant the steamer touched its wharf at this point three guides came on board, sought out the Governor, held a brief interview with him, caught up our luggage and quickly passed from the boat to the shore, where they were completely enveloped in darkness, as there were no lights on the wharf and the steamboat was but dimly lighted. It was, therefore, difficult for us to follow these guides to the hotel where we had determined to spend the remainder of the night. The darkness was so intense that even after our eyes had become accustomed to the changed condition due to our passage from the badly-lighted boat to the absolutely unlighted streets of the frontier village, our guides, though preceding us only a few paces, were still completely invisible. It was during this trying period that the chief ingeniously came to our assistance by uttering from time to time shrill war-whoops, which at this moment recalled to the mind of the Scribe the doings and sufferings of the former inhabitants of this land,—the ancient Hurons.

Having reached the hotel, we were conducted to the bar-room and office, which was dimly lighted with a single kerosene lamp. This light rendered visible the forms and faces of our guides, and consequently enabled us to form our own ideas of the persons with whom we were expected to associate during the next few days.

We now saw standing before us our three guides. The

leader was a man of small stature, about thirty-five years of age, with an erect figure and rather active in his movements. This man, whose name would probably have been written "Böttcher" had he been unfortunate enough to be born in Germany, we will now designate as John.

The chief guide was accompanied by a young brother, only seventeen years old, who was to go with us. This boy was small in figure, resembled somewhat his brother, and will hereafter on these pages be mentioned by the name of Frank. The third, a man standing about six feet without shoes, erect figure, well proportioned in every part of the body, with a glossy black face, curly black hair, flat nose, and projecting heels, was certainly the largest man in our party, and proved a very efficient and honest guide.

We will christen this man "Jim," and let the reader be assured that although his skin was black he was in every other respect "white." During his stay with us we found him at all times faithful in the discharge of his duties and likewise strictly honorable, preferring to be discharged from our service rather than that we should be balked in our efforts to obtain sport. It was settled in this bar-room, prior to our retiring to our rooms for sleep, that we should start at an early hour the next morning for Baysville, a little hamlet situated on the south branch of the Muskoka River, near "Lake of Bays." This beautiful lake is situated about fourteen miles northeast of Bracebridge and one mile from Baysville.

The chief guide had strongly recommended this lake; had spoken of it as the "sportsman's paradise"; and it afterwards was made plain to our minds that he, at least, enjoyed some especial pleasures in this land, which for complete happiness did not, however, require the use of either gun or rod.

We learned from our guides that we could reach our destination either by land or water: the canoes could be employed to transport us with our baggage through the south branch of the Muskoka River, but it would be more expeditious to take a wagon at Bracebridge, place the three canoes and other impedimenta in it, drive over the rough wood road to Baysville, and then take passage by the river to the lake.

The next morning found our party, with the exception of the guides, fully prepared for the start at an early hour. The latter were now busy in gathering in the canoes, provisions, etc. It was probably about eleven o'clock when we left the hotel. The day was pleasant, the sun shone brightly; the almost continuous cries of the blue jay were the only sounds emanating from the forest. The country traversed was very hilly; large rocks were found in the wood road; deep ravines were spanned by stilted corduroy bridges, which swayed from side to side as our wagon passed over them. Furthermore, as if to add to the excitement of the journey, one of the horses in the team which had been hired for this occasion was both vicious and balky, and seemed to enjoy kicking even better than eating. The Governor, whose peculiarities have already been mentioned, seemed greatly to prefer walking to riding this day, a fact that may be partially explained by informing the reader that the only seat provided in the wagon was in close proximity to the vicious heels, which were handled with great dexterity. The day passed on; many halts were made to rest the team, and during one of these the Scribe went a short distance into the woods, where he shot a pair of wild pigeons and soon returned with them to the wagon. We reached Baysville about one hour before sunset: the canoes were promptly placed in the water and found to be leaking badly; but there was now no time for repairs, for we were anxious to reach our destination as soon as possible in order to make ready for spending the night on a point of land near where the river comes to the lake. I have already said that the canoes were leaking badly, but this gives the reader an entirely inadequate idea of their true condition. They were certainly unfit for service, —old, broken, rotten birch structures. The guides proportioned the luggage to the supposed carrying capacity of the frail barks: guns, dogs, rods, and blankets were placed in position, and then we were told to seat ourselves, each in the stern and on the bottom of the canoe which had been previously assigned to us. It should be understood that each gentleman in the party was provided with a separate canoe, which was managed by an individual guide. Frank had charge of the vessel carrying the Governor, Jim was with Esculapius, and John paddled for the Scribe.

Prior to taking our departure from Baysville each gentleman in the party had been provided with a dish for the purpose of dipping out the water which found its way into these leaky vessels. It was found, however, impossible to keep them afloat more than a few moments at any time even by the most energetic action on our part. The guides, therefore, kept close in to the river-bank, and when it became apparent that a canoe would soon sink it was quickly paddled to the shore, drawn upon the dry land and the water emptied out. Let the kind reader now imagine himself seated in such a craft as I have just described, under the same circumstances, and I think he will fully excuse me if I say nothing about the condition of our clothing, etc.

"Say nothing about the condition of our clothing."

During this short journey from Baysville to the lake our sturdy friend Esculapius completely lost his patience, and pitched a poor little water-spaniel off the canoe into the water. This was a dog that the guides had borrowed for us at Bracebridge, that we might at least have some canine company while hunting partridges. The poor dog did not have much reputation as an assistant in hunting, but I really think he must have possessed a great deal of dignity, inasmuch as he never showed himself in our presence again.

Esculapius was very frequently reminded of this sad

event while we were in the woods, but his spirited reply was that he could not allow his own life to be jeopardized by any dog. The Governor remained silent during most of this journey, but his countenance expressed disgust, and we do not believe he has yet sufficiently recovered to speak patiently of these occurrences.

In due time we arrived at the designated spot where we were to spend the night. We saw now a small clearing, possibly about two acres of meadow-land, and in the clearing there had been erected, near the lake-shore, a small frame barn. Prior to our arrival the grass growing on this field had been cut and gathered into this building, prepared for its reception. The sun was still shining; an enchanting view was spread out before us. Here were the clear waters of an inland lake, probably about ten miles in length, and varying in width from one-half to nearly three miles, surrounded with hills which were covered with virgin forest; while as yet there were only two or three small clearings visible to us from the point where we had halted for the night. The lake-shore at this point was sandy, wood convenient, and all of the essential conditions for a pleasant camp. The entire party, including guides, were not slow to leave their bath-tubs,—so-called birch-bark canoes,—and no regrets were expressed that we were once more on land. The luggage was quickly removed and placed in such a position as to favor drying, a process which was still further aided by starting a fire. The tent with which our party was provided, a fine commodious one, was finally erected after a protest on the part of our chief guide, who declared that it was entirely unnecessary, as we could sleep so nicely on the fresh hay in the barn. The proposition to sleep in the barn was opposed by the Scribe, an old soldier, who expressed a decided preference for a bed of balsam boughs beneath the clean canvas; but the Governor and Esculapius favored the proposition made by John, who was supposed by them to know very well what was best for us under these circumstances; therefore the tent was employed, while we remained at this point, only as a baggage- and mess-room. The tent having been erected and a fire built, the labor next in order was the preparation, by the guides, of the evening meal, which consisted of broiled ham, broiled pigeon, bread, butter, and tea.

The labors of the day had prepared us for the full enjoyment of this meal, which was followed by the free use of cigars, which we had brought with us. We sat about the camp-fire, smoking and chatting, for several hours after the darkness had gathered in about us.

The guides, having gathered wood for the camp-fire, and performed such other duties as were required of them for the time being, with our consent crossed the lake in their canoes, for the purpose of visiting a family living in a log cabin distant from our camp about two miles. We subsequently discovered that the principal attraction for our guides in this cabin was its fair and rather famous hostess, who seemed to be equally appreciated by the chief and his colored companion, Jim. It was about nine o'clock when the Governor, Esculapius, and the Scribe entered the barn, spread their blankets on the hay, and sought refreshment in sleep. Towards morning their slumbers were rudely disturbed by the entrance of the guides, who were talking and laughing joyfully, being in no manner restrained in their merriment by the presence of those whom they had engaged to serve. Blankets were entirely discarded by them; they threw themselves down on the hay without removing any portion of their wardrobes. The Governor and his companions now discovered that the hay on which they were reposing was not quite equal to a spring-bed covered with a hair-mattress. Deep holes had formed at various points beneath them; they had slipped from their blankets, on which they had intended to repose; their hair and clothing had become filled with hay-seed, etc.; and the advantages of the barn, which had been so glowingly described to them by Chief John, were not fully realized. The Governor never winced under these peculiarly trying circumstances, a fact that has always been regarded by the Scribe as a marvellous manifestation of patience and fortitude on the part of one wholly unaccustomed to hardships. Esculapius came to the front in the morning smiling and happy. He evidently cared but little for the trifling annoyance arising from hay-seed and the irregular surface of the bed on which he had attempted to sleep; it had not endangered his life; it could not be compared with the danger that had threatened his life on the preceding day, when he had so cheerfully parted company with the little dog. The Scribe was not pleased with these sleeping accommodations; knew that they might be improved; but then there was some consolation in the thought that he had suffered much less in this situation than the Governor.

Our arrival at the camp had taken place on Saturday evening, and consequently our first breakfast was partaken of on Sunday morning, while we were seated around the camp-fire at about nine o'clock. This meal had been promptly prepared by our guides as their first duty in the morning, but the next thing in order was the pitching of their leaky canoes,—a labor that engaged their attention about two hours.

Scarcely had this work been completed when the loud baying of the hound—the only dog now remaining with the party—was heard in the swamp not far distant from our camp. This hound had been extravagantly praised by Chief John, the owner, during our short acquaintance with him, but I think every other person in the party was inclined to look on him as a worthless animal. The chief now shouted to us joyfully, "Hear the music; get your guns; my hound is running a deer. I wish to station you on the run-ways coming into the lake." His orders were obeyed with alacrity; we were stationed; all were joyful; but it was soon apparent from the sounds emitted by the hound that he was running in small circles, neither leaving nor approaching the lake, and could not, therefore, be chasing a deer, which never runs in this manner, but was unquestionably running a rabbit. The chief guide called us away from the run-ways, after having kept us there about an hour. While standing around the camp-fire immediately after our return from the run-ways, Jim said to Chief John, "Your dog was chasing a rabbit and not a deer." The chief replied, "I have never known him to do so before." It was, however, subsequently admitted by the owner that the dog had never been trained; had never been tried in the forest on any game; and permit me to say that many subsequent trials demonstrated to us his entire worthlessness. He could not be made to run a deer. The further doings of the day consisted in the taking of a three-pound speckled trout and the shooting of two wood-ducks by the Scribe. The taking of this beautiful fish came near causing us serious trouble, in consequence of its having been reported to the fish-warden, who followed us several miles down the lake to a new camp, where he was persuaded by the cautious, able, and accomplished ambassador, the Governor, to compromise the whole case, thus possibly avoiding international complications. It was an undeniable fact that the fish had been caught on Sunday, in violation of the Canadian laws. This law makes no allowance in favor of the hungry foreign sportsman. There was shot, by Esculapius, during the same day a ruffed grouse, which had come into our camp apparently for the purpose of taking a survey of camp-luggage, etc. I am not absolutely certain that this feat was performed by Esculapius; the Governor may possibly have had some hand in it, but I believe that Esculapius claimed the honor. Sunday night was spent by the whole party in the same manner as Saturday night. We again attempted to sleep on the hay; the guides again visited their fair hostess, and returned to us at a late hour apparently very happy. The next morning we were stirring early,—had been promised by Chief John that he would this day lead us into the sportsman's paradise. In answer to our inquiries he said, "This promised land is situated only about six miles from here, and there you will find an abundance of deer, fowl, and trout." The Governor, who is an expert fisherman, throws the fly most skilfully, and at the same time with charming grace, was highly delighted with the glowing description to which he had listened, and, therefore, took his departure from the barn in anticipation of the great pleasure just about to be realized. The morning meal had been made ready and ample justice done to the viands placed before us. The luggage belonging to the party was closely packed and stowed away in the canoes. The chief had taken the Governor into his canoe for the trip down the lake, Frank had charge of Esculapius, and Jim paddled for the Scribe. This arrangement, I think, had been effected by the chief guide, who probably thought it necessary that he should now impress the Governor with his own importance and skill in order that the leader of our hunting-party might be made a firm supporter of all his plans. This arrangement for our journey afforded the Scribe an opportunity to question our colored guide in regard to the best localities on the lake for fishing and hunting. He had previously observed that Jim was not well at ease while John was describing the advantages for sport of the spot towards which we were now steering our frail barks. Jim approached the subject with, apparently, a full appreciation of the duty which he owed to our party and likewise to his superior, John. He had allowed a few careless remarks to fall from his lips while standing about our camp-fire. I now plied him with questions, which he finally answered with frankness. He said, in substance, "You will find no game of any sort that you will be willing to shoot or hook anywhere near the point to which he is conducting you." I then asked, "What object has John in deceiving us in this matter?" The reply was given after a little hesitation, but without any marked effort at evasion. I cannot attempt to recall Jim's words, but they were, in effect, as follows: "John is a widower; he lost his first wife some years ago; he wishes to remarry, and is courting a girl who lives with her parents in the bush about one mile from the unoccupied shanty to which he is now conducting you. He wishes to spend much of his time in the company of this girl. He thinks you are green, and that he can fool you into staying there while he is courting at your expense. I would like to see you have good sport, but you will find none there." This statement was made with a certain degree of confidence to me, and I quickly determined to make no use of it at present, but to wait until it had been verified by our own experience. Only a few days at most would be required for this purpose.

Our canoe was now passing the mouth of Watte's Creek. Jim remarked to me that this creek afforded the best trout-fishing on the lake. "I am not a professional guide," he said, "but am acquainted with every person living on this lake; have worked as a wood-chopper a great deal about here; all these people fish and hunt more or less, and I have frequently fished and hunted with them." I inquired still further about Watte's Creek as a fishing locality. Jim said he thought there might be some ducks and pigeons in that vicinity, likewise adding that he would like to remain there one day with me; thought I might kill a considerable number of ducks if I could shoot them on the wing. I preferred, however, to continue on in company with the Governor and Esculapius, thinking that I might now be of some service to them, and was determined that neither John nor the girl in the bush should prevent us from securing some sport on the lake. In due time we reached the lake-shore in front of the shanty in which John's inamorata resided; the canoes were soon drawn on the dry land, and the chief proudly led us into the log structure which contained the fair damsel whose magnetic influence over our guide seemed to betoken nothing but disappointment and vexation for us. The maiden's mother was at this moment the only occupant of the little room to which John had conducted us. She received us kindly, invited us to be seated, and we all complied with this invitation, including even our guides, with the exception of our wily chief, who left the room in search of his fair lady, whom he unquestionably soon discovered, guided by that unerring influence that we have already mentioned. It was now about two o'clock; we partook of a lunch in this shanty, the hostess contributing to it bread and milk; our party were now refreshed and ready for new triumphs. The Governor asked to be conducted to the fishing-grounds. Frank was directed to accompany him, John having given his brother the necessary instructions for finding the place.

The Governor has made a selection of flies for use this afternoon from the book in which he carries a large supply. He has likewise examined his beautiful rod, and finally declared himself fully prepared for pleasure. His face is wreathed in a pleasant smile, his heart is

beating joyously in anticipation of coming events. He has
started for the famous trout stream so vividly described to
him by John as one of the tributaries of this lake. Esculapius and the Scribe now hold a brief consultation with
John for the purpose of determining what shall be done
by the rest of the party during the afternoon. John thinks
it would be just as well to rest until morning and then take
a fresh start. This did not suit the party, and it was finally
proposed that Jim should take the luggage in a canoe, go
to the unoccupied shanty, situated about a mile from this
point, and prepare the same for our occupation. Neither
the Governor nor Esculapius are yet willing to sleep under
canvas if it can be avoided. Jim is promptly off for the
performance of the duty assigned to him. John is to guide
Esculapius and the Scribe through the woods in search of
partridge. We have selected our shells, donned our hunting-coats, and with our guns in hand are ready to be off
at the word from John, who left us only a few moments
ago, possibly to give a parting salute to the magnet which
now controlled him. After an absence of fifteen or twenty
minutes he returned to us and declared his readiness to
lead us. We started into the woods, he leading at a very
rapid pace, while we followed as rapidly as possible. It
required only a few moments for him to distance us. We
called to him to wait; he halted, but only permitted us to
approach within easy speaking distance before he was off
again, this time on a slow trot. We called to him once
more; this time he allowed us to approach somewhat nearer
to him, but showed much uneasiness; was apparently just
ready to be off again when we checked these indications

by a united request for a rest. We now took seats on a log; were bathed in perspiration and blowing like a wind-broken horse. We ventured to remonstrate with him for travelling so rapidly; suggested that he had kept so far ahead of us that had he discovered game, as he was not provided with a gun, the birds would in all probability have escaped before a shot could be fired. He told us that he was a very fast traveller; was not walking this afternoon as rapidly as usual, but would try to moderate his pace to suit us. We soon started again; he travelled now faster than before. We walked and ran in our efforts to keep up to him, but found it impossible. This chase was continued about three hours, when we halted in front of the log cabin which he intended we should occupy during the night. This tramp was one long to be remembered, and sufficiently severe to deter any one from entering the woods for the purpose of hunting, if he believed such exercise was required, but we knew it to be unnecessary and inconsistent with any success. The Governor arrived in front of the cabin a few moments after we reached it. His face was bathed in perspiration, almost livid with rage, and he directed his eyes towards John, who had just seated himself on a log near the cabin door. John probably felt the force of this piercing look, as he meekly inquired, "Did you find the stream which I described to you?" We found the dry bed of a mountain stream, but I don't believe there ever was water enough in it to cover a three-pound trout, except during the early spring when the snow is melting. Our whole party was tired, disappointed, and disgusted with the conduct of John. The colored guide, Jim, had opened the door of the cabin and found it contained a large quantity of odoriferous, mouldering hay, which had been left behind by the last occupants, who had vacated it about nine months before our arrival. The entire cabin consisted of a single room, which was probably about twelve feet square and lighted by a single pane of glass. This diminutive window could not be readily opened or removed. It was still closed when Esculapius, who had entered the room, quickly retired, declaring that the stench arising from the decomposition was unendurable.

He directed that the hay should be removed, the small window forced open; all of which was promptly done by Jim and Frank, while John was resting on the log, where he had seated himself on his arrival before the cabin. Let it suffice to say that after improving the atmospheric condition of the cabin as much as practicable, the Governor and Esculapius determined to occupy it as their sleeping-apartment during the night, while the Scribe preferred to remain outside, sleeping on the ground with no other protection than that afforded by the pure air and a cloudless sky. The guides had withdrawn from us during the early part of the evening, returning to the cabin containing John's enchantress.

## CHAPTER III.

GRAND FISHING EXCURSION—WATTE'S CREEK VISITED BY THE GOVERNOR AND ESCULAPIUS—THEIR RETURN AND RECEPTION AT CAMP—GRAND DEER-HUNT, LED BY DR. POKORNEY—CHIEF JOHN AND HIS ASSISTANTS ARE RELIEVED FROM DUTY AND GO TO THE REAR IN DISGRACE—DR. POKORNEY AND OTHER ASSISTANTS.

IT was about four o'clock in the morning when the Governor emerged from his unsavory sleeping-apartment with a haggard face and despondent heart. I had slept soundly during the greater part of the night; was now greatly refreshed and ready to engage with him in conversation. The Governor, when he discovered that I was awake, remarked, "I have never spent a more miserable night; the atmosphere of the cabin is stifling. I am sick this morning. I think we had better start for home; I have had enough of this sort of sport." I then revealed to him the fact that had been confided to me by Jim. I spoke to him of the fine trout-fishing which could be had in Watte's Creek. He seemed, at first, somewhat incredulous in regard to the statements made to me on the previous day by Jim, but finally the real motives controlling the acts of the chief guide became apparent to him.  I had suggested that the Governor and Esculapius, with Jim and Frank, start immediately for Watte's Creek; that I remain behind with John; that during the absence of my friends I would, with the assistance of John, put up the tent, make all necessary arrangements for their comfort and a deer-hunt, which should follow promptly after their return.  It required considerable urging on my part to bring this part of my programme into force, but soon after daylight Esculapius came from the cabin; he too was sick,—was discouraged, but when I had explained our present intentions, and all the facts connected with the same, he readily consented to its adoption.  In the mean time the guides having arrived, breakfast has been eaten, the Governor and Esculapius, with the guides, Jim and Frank, are off for the fishing-ground.  John remains behind with me.  He seems tired, is ill-natured; declares that neither the Governor nor Esculapius will find any sport at Watte's Creek.

It was after considerable urging that I succeeded in getting him to take hold with me and put up the tent; but this was finally accomplished, and then the balsam boughs were arranged in true Adirondack style.  The bed and tent were all that a sportsman could wish.  I once more requested John to lead me in the woods.  He was a little slow in getting off and very slow after he had got off.  During a short ramble in the woods to-day I shot a partridge and a very large porcupine.  The following night I was alone in camp,—John had gone to the same cabin where he had spent the last night, and was not seen again until the next morning. The night was passed in refreshing slumber; the weather had been delightful since we left Bracebridge,—no rain. The following day was spent about camp. John now admitted to me that his hound was worthless and would not run deer. Jim had previously informed me that there was an excellent deer-hunter living on the lake-shore, about three miles from our camp. He also said that this man owned an excellent deer-hound and would be very glad to give us some sport. Soon after John entered the camp I engaged him in a conversation relating to our proposed deer-hunt. He was not so ill-natured this morning as he had been during the past two days, and said, frankly, "My dog is worthless; we can't hunt deer without a good dog. I know of only one about this lake, and that is owned by an old Polander, who lives three miles from here." I then asked, "Can you not hire this dog a few days?" John replied, "No; the old doctor is very poor, has a large family, and supports them by hunting; the dog is so necessary to him that he will not allow it to go out of his sight; but he is friendly with me, and I think he will join us in a deer-hunt if we give him about three dollars a day. This would secure for us the use of the best deer-hound on this lake." I replied, "Let us employ him immediately." This conversation occurred while John was busied with the preparation for breakfast, and when the meal had been eaten and the odd jobs about the camp performed to my satisfaction I urged John to go in search of the old deer-hunter, Dr. Pokorney, and bring him to me. John was now perfectly willing to aid me in arranging for a deer-hunt; he was evidently in better spirits that morning than he had been at any time since we left the camp near the barn. The attempt to deceive us and bring us into quiet subjection had completely failed. He fully realized at this moment that his original plan had completely miscarried, and had recovered from the shock arising from this disappointment. I walked to the lake with John when he started out to find Dr. Pokorney.

He placed the little bark in the water, stepped lightly into it, assumed a position on his knees,—the one which is always taken by the Indian or backwoodsman who is to paddle the canoe,—and was off with a light heart. After an absence of three or four hours he returned to me with the joyful intelligence that the old deer-hunter would be with us in our camp within a few hours. He had found him at his cabin, busied in stopping, with wood and mud, the holes existing between the logs, which, in the summer, were not objectionable, but which must be carefully closed before the approach of the cold Canadian winter. In accordance with the promise which the deer-hunter had made to John, he was in our camp before three o'clock in the afternoon. The object which had prompted me to seek this interview was immediately stated to him. He replied, "I am entirely at your service." I then informed him that I had two companions who were now temporarily absent, but who, I thought, would rejoin me in the evening and be ready to participate with us in the hunt the next day. He said, "I learned these facts from John to-day, and I will be here to-morrow morning at six o'clock to start the hunt."

The intelligence shown by Dr. Pokorney in this conversation had greatly surprised me. John had spoken of him as "a doctor," but I had only thought of him in connection with this title as an ignorant quack. I now found myself in the presence of a well-educated gentleman, who was also evidently familiar with the rules governing polite society. He conversed with me in the English language, but I soon learned that he could also speak both German and French. You can, therefore, well imagine my surprise: here was a gentleman possessed of an excellent education—a professional man—living in a cold, rocky, sterile country, with no congenial associates, while the few other settlers on this lake could only be classed with ignorant adventurers, some of whom freely admitted that they left the front in order to avoid confinement in prisons. The doctor seemed to be about fifty years of age, was thinly clad, stooped considerably, while his shoulders drooped, and there were likewise observed other evidences of continued hardships and scanty nourishment. He was tall and gaunt, stood, probably, about six feet in his boots, sunken gray eyes, heavy eyebrows, light complexion, iron-gray hair, and heavy moustache. The mystery of the man's life is still unknown to me. He was certainly an enthusiastic hunter, and may he not have parted with the pleasures of civilization for the purpose of enjoying the wild pleasures of the forest? I cannot answer this question. We found him there on the "Free Grant Lands," working hard to support a large family, scarcely able to put bread in their mouths, staggering under the heavy burden imposed on him, and with very little hope for a better condition on earth.

The first meeting with Dr. Pokorney was a great surprise to me. It is true, I had expected to meet this well-known deer-hunter, but I had not expected to meet such a man. He remained with me in camp, I think, about two or three hours, and then returned to the place that he called home. The Governor and Esculapius, in accordance with my expectations, returned to our camp this evening. The tent is now in perfect order; the fragrant balsamic odor which pervades it proclaims the presence of a couch worthy to receive the body of a king. The camp-fire burned brightly a few feet in front of it and lighted up everything about it. The necessary amount of wood has been gathered in and piled near at hand, so that this beautiful fire, which is the charming source of light, may be continued all night if desired by the campers. Our camp is situated near the lake-shore. It was about nine o'clock when we heard the merry sound of approaching voices. Listen one moment: Jim is singing, and that sounds like the Governor's happy laugh. Esculapius has discovered our camp-fire; hear his joyful shout, "Hallo there!" Both John and I are on our feet, peering out on the lake, —it is a calm night; it is moonlight,—we can barely make out in the distance the two little canoes which are approaching our camp. We shout back to our friends; shout answers shout; and they quickly touch the shore at our feet. Behold the beautiful sight: there lay in the bottom of these canoes not less than forty speckled beauties, not one of which weighed less than one pound, and many weighed four. We greeted each other with a hearty hand-shaking. The Governor recounted to me the same evening the pleasures of this trip, and I now participated with him in the enjoyment he had felt while catching these fish.

He is an enthusiastic fisherman, but cares little for shooting. Esculapius seemed to be perfectly satisfied with the part which he had taken in this little excursion; admitted that he had fired a great number of shots at ducks and pigeons, but showed us no game.

The tent now presented to the Governor and Esculapius an attractive appearance, and they entered it without uttering a single demurrer. We all slept soundly under the canvas, inhaled the pure atmosphere of the forest, and awoke early in the morning with renewed energies and pleasant forebodings for the day.

The deer-hunter, Dr. Pokorney, reached our camp about six o'clock that morning; was immediately introduced to the Governor and Esculapius. He seemed this morning to be in excellent spirits. The Governor exhibited to him some of the speckled beauties with much apparent satisfaction.

The guides soon announced that breakfast was ready, and it did not take many minutes for our whole party to arrange themselves in a semicircle on the ground around the spot where it had been decided to place the meal. A rubber poncho had been placed on the ground, and it was on this small blanket that the cups containing the smoking hot coffee and the plates laden with the fried fish and boiled potatoes were placed.

The whole party, including Dr. Pokorney, ate heartily, and every one, including John, seemed well pleased. The breakfast is ended, and the Governor, who is provided with pipes and tobacco, brings out his entire stock. There is now placed before our new-made friend, Dr. Pokorney,

48                    THE SPORTSMAN'S PARADISE;

Swallowing fish and fish-stories.

at least a half-dozen fresh brier-wood pipes and several pounds of tobacco. He is invited to make a selection and proceed to the next order of business, which is smoking. He, being able to decide with promptness on all such matters, was soon afterwards seen in the full enjoyment of his pipe. Esculapius had followed suit, but the Scribe was so unfortunate as to be unable to join them in this pleasant pastime. The Governor having supplied the wants of the party, now drew from an inside pocket of his coat a case containing a beautifully colored meerschaum pipe, which he leisurely proceeded to fill, and afterwards quietly smoked.

A heavy white frost covered every bush and exposed surface of earth or rock. However, there is only a light breeze, and, therefore, the lake is comparatively smooth. It is a grand morning for a deer-hunt: the bucks are moving in such weather at this season of the year. It was nearly nine o'clock before our party was ready to embark in their canoes for that portion of the lake where it had been decided that the deer-hunt should take place. The locality of the hunt had been chosen by Dr. Pokorney, although some suggestions had been made by John. These suggestions had been entirely ignored by the old deer-hunter, who did not seem to think them worthy of his consideration. He, however, did inform us that the locality was chosen with due regard to the wind and other factors involved in the practical solution of the question. When we started from the shore in front of our camp Dr. Pokorney was in his own canoe, accompanied by his deer-hound; the Governor followed in a canoe with John; Esculapius was accompanied by Jim, while Frank was paddling for me. These old, leaky canoes, which I have previously described, have been somewhat improved, it is true, by the pitch that has been employed to stop the leaks, but we are still compelled to use, very frequently, the dishes to keep the water to a point consistent with our own safety, while we are still obliged to sit in a cold-water bath. I have observed that Dr. Pokorney's birch-bark canoe is nearly new and does not leak, while by a graceful and apparently easy use of the paddle it shoots over the water with great rapidity. The comparison of the old hunter's canoe with those which John has supplied for our use is not well calculated to make us feel contented while quietly seated in cold water. Let us, however, dismiss from our minds, for the present, these unpleasant thoughts, and again resume the details of the deer-hunt. Dr. Pokorney took the lead in his canoe at the start, and paddled away from the camp about three miles, having kept in advance all this time before he stationed the Governor at a run-way where it came to the lake. The point which the Governor was to watch having been selected by the deer-hunter, John immediately brought his canoe to the shore, when both parties occupying it stepped to the dry land, while the guide promptly removed the water which it contained. Dr. Pokorney beckoned to the occupants of the other canoes to follow him, which they continued to do. He now proceeded on about one-half mile farther, where he stationed the Scribe and Frank, and about one mile from them he placed Esculapius with the colored guide. Our whole party were now stationed, and everything was in readiness to start the hound which was expected to drive the deer into the lake. This animal had remained in the canoe with its master since we left our camp in the morning, and as soon as our party were properly stationed the old deer-hunter paddled back near to the spot where he had left the Scribe, in full view of whom he drew his bark canoe on the shore. The dog immediately leaped from the frail bark and began to run playfully around his master's feet, looking anxiously up to his face. Dr. Pokorney spoke kindly to the animal, petted her a moment, and then bade her to bring a deer. She started immediately, ran off a few rods and then halted, as if to receive further instructions, turned partially around, and again gazed into her master's face. He again urged her on, and pointed at the same time in the direction which he desired her to take. She now leaped forward into the woods, giving at the same moment a single yelp, and was lost to our vision. Nothing more was heard from her until after the lapse of nearly an hour, when we again faintly heard the music of her voice. Nearer, still nearer, are these sounds; clearer, still clearer, are they heard by us on the lake. Listen, her voice is now becoming fainter: she is evidently leaving the lake; the deer which she is running has turned back: he is making a circle. "Never mind," remarked the old hunter, "she will run him so sharply that he will certainly come to water; you will hear her voice again soon." Scarcely half an hour had elapsed when we again heard her voice; faint at first, but more and more and more distinct every succeeding moment. Onward she steadily went; she was almost at the lake. A splash was heard on our right, a few seconds later one was heard on our left; Frank whispered, "Take your place in the canoe." He pushed the little bark from the sand to the water, and I promptly seated myself in the bow. Frank paddled noiselessly out into the lake, while we scanned the water both to the right and left. After the lapse of a few moments we discovered a buck's head, which was held above the water on our right. The animal was swimming away from the shore and towards the middle of the lake. He had not yet discovered us, and we desired to place our canoe between the swimming deer and the lake-shore in order to prevent him from returning to the woods before we could get sufficiently near to take a shot. Frank now allowed our canoe to float quietly; the deer was still making towards the centre of the lake. We waited patiently; the deer was now a half-mile from the shore where he had entered the water. The lake at this point is about two miles in width. We were now ready for the chase; we can cut him off from the shore where he entered and kill him before he can cross the lake. Frank handed me a spare paddle which he had in readiness in the canoe. The bark is headed, and we both pull away with all our might. The deer has discovered us: *behold his frantic efforts.*

He has turned his head towards the shore and is making his greatest efforts to avoid this new danger; he has evaded the dog when he reached the water, but the chase has been taken up by a more dangerous enemy.

"He has evaded the dog, but——"

He is now completely foiled: the canoe has come between him and the shore where he entered; he turns once more his head towards the centre of the lake. He has made his last great effort; his doom is sealed. The Scribe has dropped his paddle into the bottom of the canoe and picked up his gun. Frank pulled steadily towards the deer and gained rapidly. A few moments later a white puff of smoke arose over the canoe; the deer dropped his head and floated motionless in the water, while the sound of the discharge of the gun in the hands of the Scribe echoed around the lake. Scarcely had the reverberations died away when another shot was heard on our right; still another: the Governor was at work. He, too, had killed a deer, while we afterwards learned that the third had run the shore in front of Esculapius, but he was too much surprised to even fire a shot at this animal. The canoes now came together on the lake; we greeted each other warmly; everybody was happy once more.

It was now about two o'clock in the afternoon, and we quickly decided to go to our camp. The day had been passed very pleasantly by us and we had been rewarded with success. I have hunted very frequently since that day, but have never seen three deer driven to water by a single dog in a single run since that time. We continued to hunt deer several days—a week or more—with Dr. Pokorney and his wonderful dog. This animal continued to manifest the same intelligence; was sent into the woods in the same manner each day by her master, and rarely failed to bring a deer to the water. This dog would probably not attract much attention at a bench show, although I have never seen her equal in the field. She was a dark liver-and-white female hound, called by her master "Fan;" he did not know or even care anything about her pedigree. This grand animal was rather large when compared with the deer-hounds that I have been accustomed to see, and also unusually long and lank; possessed of pleasant, sunken eyes. She, like her master, was accustomed to work, and certainly was not overfed. Having reached our camp, the deer-hunter set to work and quickly dressed both deer, which were left hanging out of the reach of the dogs. The other guides gathered the wood and prepared the evening meal, which we will designate as our dinner, inasmuch as we had not partaken of food since the early morning. Our repast consisted of trout, venison, coffee, etc., and it is scarcely necessary to say that it was thoroughly enjoyed by our whole party. Having completed the meal, and while the Governor, Esculapius, and Dr. Pokorney were smoking their pipes, the question was raised, What shall we do to-morrow? Another deer-hunt was finally determined on, in which Dr. Pokorney and his faithful dog Fan were to participate. John now excused himself, and hastened away to report the day's proceedings to his inamorata, while the old deer-hunter remained with us until the sun had disappeared behind the western hills, when he bade us good-evening and started for his cabin.

The next morning Dr. Pokorney was with us about six o'clock. John reached our camp about the same hour. He was evidently not in the most agreeable frame of mind: something must have gone wrong since he parted from us last evening. It is now evident that he intends to direct the future movements of the whole party. He has informed Dr. Pokorney that the hunt to-day ought to take place at a certain point on the lake; they find themselves unable to agree on this subject, when the Governor came to the aid of the latter, and poor John was thus left in the minority. He could not good-naturedly endure all this, and remained sullen during the whole day. *Poor unhappy man!* What is the matter with you? Are you in love, and loved and still unhappy? How are we to explain your conduct? We have carefully studied your case, and have also pondered seriously the doctrine of the transmigrations as propounded by Pythagoras, and ask now the question, Has not the soul of some departed Huron chief found a temporary lodgment within the body of this unhappy man? But the more we studied the antics of this curious fellow the more puzzling became the solution of the questions. Chief John was not a lover of "fire-water," but with this exception, his light, quick, and elastic step, keen sight, acute sense of hearing, extensive knowledge of wood-craft, all proclaimed the ruling spirit of the noble red man, and our guide in his own words assured us that he possessed all these; nevertheless there was something wonderfully conflicting between his words and acts. It was during the second day of the deer-hunt, led by Dr. Pokorney, that the Governor declared, in the presence of the Scribe, that inasmuch as "a house divided against itself cannot stand," therefore John must take his departure.

It was evident to us that the Governor had reached this conclusion after much patient thought; but since the conduct of the guides associated with him had been entirely satisfactory to us, the important question that now arose was, How shall they be treated in this emergency? The Governor held an interview with Jim, explained to him the situation, and it was amicably arranged between them that the latter and also Frank should go back with John to Bracebridge. In accordance with this treaty, John and his assistants departed from our camp the same evening. It was evident to all observers that this difficult and embarrassing negotiation had been conducted with masterly skill on the part of our ambassador, since even John seemed satisfied and but slightly crestfallen when he parted from us. Jim urged us to come back into this country once more and give him a chance to act as our chief guide, —a position which we all knew he would fill to our entire satisfaction, since he had at all times, while in our service, acted in good faith and with a true regard to our comforts and best interests. Dr. Pokorney had been consulted by the Governor before he took this decisive action, and had informed the latter that he could immediately supply the required number of assistants, canoes, etc.; in fact, two colored men in new birch-bark canoes reported at our camp within an hour after John's departure.

The change was found to be highly agreeable. The new canoes afforded us a dry, warm seat while we were on the lake, instead of reposing continually in a cold-water bath, as we had previously done. Dr. Pokorney now brought into camp with him his son in addition to the parties which I have previously mentioned. The son remained in camp, took charge of the fire and tent while the father and the other guides were engaged with us in the deer-hunting. We were never left in camp without attendants. These guides remained with us night and day, although they were unprovided with tents or other shelter than their canoes. I frequently saw them sit with their backs supported by trees, sleeping soundly while their clothing was thoroughly drenched with water and the rain still pouring down on them. Their canoes, when turned bottom side up,—bows placed on a log or rock so as to admit air and light,—afforded them very fair protection against a storm, while the space beneath them was ample to enable them to turn or move as much as was necessary during sleeping hours.

The attendance in camp and the guidance while in search of game was now all that we could wish. We found Dr. Pokorney well versed in deer-hunting, and at the same time intelligent and companionable. His son, a lad of sixteen, brave and hardy, frequently amused me by the narration of his exploits in the Canadian forests at mid-winter, while engaged as a companion to an old beaver-trapper. His story, although not entirely new, was indeed very interesting. The boy said, "It was in the latter part of the month of January that I started, in company with old Ben, to go back into the bush about seventy-five miles in order to trap beaver. The weather was very cold and the snow was nearly three feet deep, and we were compelled to use snow-shoes. The hardest part of our work consisted in carrying in our provisions, traps, and other things required in trapping. When we started from this lake I carried a pack which weighed about fifty pounds. The first day out we travelled about ten miles, halted for the night and cleared the snow from a space large enough for the fire and our bed. The required amount of wood and the balsam boughs were gathered, the fire built and the bed arranged, after which we prepared and ate our supper, and then wrapped ourselves in a woollen blanket, with which each was provided, and lay down for sleep." I inquired of the lad, "Were you able to sleep?" thinking the cold would probably act as a potent barrier in this instance. The reply came promptly from the hardy lad, "Oh yes! I slept very well, for Uncle Ben kept up a good fire all night." He then added, "The next morning, after breakfast, we again shouldered our packs and pushed forward about six miles into the forest, when we marked the spot and buried our luggage." In answer to my inquiry he informed me that they buried their packs, consisting of provisions and traps, to keep other trappers, who might chance to pass that way, from appropriating these articles to their own use, which might otherwise happen. The hiding having been completed, the old trapper and his assistant retraced their steps to the log cabin from which they had originally started on their journey to the woods. Here they remained only until the following morning, when they again started with other packs. This severe work of packing lasted more than two weeks, when they reached the locality that had been selected for trapping beaver. I have avoided a repetition of his daily narrative, lest it might become tiresome to the reader, although it was very interesting to me when minutely detailed by the junior participant. The story as told involved the daily doings, the exposures, hardships, and fatigues of the old backwoodsman and his youthful assistant. They were in the woods nearly three months, without the protection of even a canoe, tent, or any other shelter, during that portion of the time in which they were engaged in transporting their provisions and traps to the new field of labor. Having reached their destination they then erected huts, which they occupied as long as they remained.

Let us now return to our camp-life on the Lake of the Bays, from which we have wandered so far while speaking of Dr. Pokorney's son. We have already described the deer-hunt that occurred immediately after Dr. Pokorney joined our party, and in addition to this we have incidentally mentioned the fact that on the following day we engaged again in the same sport, which was continued day after day for more than a week with varying success, after the departure of John and his assistants. I cannot at this moment recall the number of animals killed, or the particulars of each chase, and even were I able to do so it would certainly be somewhat monotonous to the reader.

When the time came for us to start homeward, it was suggested by Dr. Pokorney that it would be more convenient for us to leave by the way of Huntsville than to retrace our steps to Baysville; and consequently we started from this lake on which we had spent a very pleasant time in the company of our guides.

We were compelled to portage our canoes and luggage from Lake of the Bays to Peninsula Lake, but we readily passed from the latter by its outlet to Fairy Lake and down this lake to Huntsville, where we parted with Dr. Pokorney and his colored assistants.

We remained at this frontier village only a few hours, having arrived in the afternoon and taking our departure the following morning by the old stage-coach, which put us down in Bracebridge the same day about sunset. The return to our homes was made without the occurrence of any important events worthy of mention here.

## CHAPTER IV.

THE START AND INCIDENTS OF THE JOURNEY—LUMBERMEN AND THEIR DRUNKEN ORGIES—TRAVELLING BY THE ROYAL MAIL STAGE IN MUSKOKA—THE PARTY ATTACKED BY FLEAS—CAMP ON CANOE LAKE—DEER-HUNTING—GOVERNOR STARTS FOR HOME—THE REMAINDER OF THE PARTY OFF FOR NEW FIELDS—CAMP ON PICKEREL LAKE—RAIN AND FISH—CROSSING THE HORKA-PORKA PORTAGE—CAMP ON ROCK LAKE—TROUT-FISHING—CAMP NEAR LOON AND GRASS LAKES—CAMP ON SAND LAKE—HOMEWARD BOUND.

WEDNESDAY, 13TH.—Arrived at the Falls of Niagara at eight A.M., and a few moments later started for Toronto, and reached that city at one-thirty P.M. Dined, and afterwards saw a display of the fire department, given in honor of the magnates of Rochester and Buffalo, who are paying a visit to the exhibition that is now being held here. The force of the water is so great that no engines are necessary; the water, rushing through the hose, ascends to the highest roof.

Afterwards we strolled through the city, admiring the beautifully laid out streets and the fine buildings. Among other scenes we visited St. James' Cathedral,—a magnificent structure,—and we ascended the spire, which is three hundred and nineteen feet high. Here a perfect panorama lay at our feet; a fine view was obtained, but it was in miniature, on account of the great height. Yachts were seen flying through the water; vessels at anchor; steamboats, of which there was a fleet, dashing to and fro. A little beyond was the home of the great sculler, who learned to row on the placid waters of the lake, which is here nearly land-locked.* At Toronto we procured camping-blankets and provisions which we would require whilst sojourning in the woods. We did not visit the exhibition, as we were anxious to drink in the ozone of the wilderness.

*Thursday, 14th.*—Started for Gravenhurst,—had a palace-car to ourselves. The conductor was extremely polite and attentive, pointing out every object of interest which we passed on the road. While our time was thus occupied, in the other car were sixteen lumbermen who were engaged to go into the woods to cut lumber,—men who held a continual drunken orgy. The bottles of whiskey were continually passing from mouth to mouth. They were the most besotted set of men it was ever my lot to encounter. However, they kept to themselves and troubled no one. Reached Gravenhurst,—a place consisting of a few houses, —and immediately took a small steamboat, at half-past one, and proceeded to the upper part of Lake Rosseau. We had dinner and supper on board, as the boat did not reach Rosseau until eight P.M. Three of the lumbermen came to the table, and we had a scene with one of them. His appetite was ravenous, and plate after plate disappeared before him. It made no difference of what it was composed. During dinner the steward called upon him for the price of his meal,—only forty cents. His reply was that he would have to wait till he was sure that he had taken enough, and again he attacked the eatables. If the rest of the band were only able to come to the table the captain would not realize much from that dinner. This man did not come to the supper-table. His appetite reminded me of an Indian at a feast, laying in a stock for several days. We stopped at Pratt's Hotel, newly gotten up and finished. The proprietor is a Bostonian; he refused the other party, who got accommodations a little below. During the night they got up and stole all the whiskey that the landlord had. Rosseau is prettily situated at the head of the lake. The hotel occupies a prominent location. The proprietor informed us that *last summer it was full* of guests from Boston and its surroundings. Mr. Pratt knows how to run a hotel, and his charges are certainly reasonable, as is shown by the fact that for bed and breakfast he demands only seventy-five cents. The hotel has since burned down; the capacity at that time being about one hundred guests.

We made arrangements with the driver of the mail to take us and our paraphernalia to Maganetawan. Our coach was a large farm-wagon without a cover and minus springs. It was pleasanter without the first, and we were on the road but a short time when we discovered why it was without the second. The road, if such it could be called, was so stony that no springs could stand the journey without being demolished. After an early breakfast the wagon drove up to the door, and one of our party opened his eyes at the prodigious turnout. He said that he would prefer a spring-wagon; so would we, but there was no alternative. Thirty-five miles had to be travelled before we reached our destination. We took our guns and rods, and the driver then informed us that with ourselves and the other passengers the load would be so heavy that he could not take our provisions, but he would send them later. We informed him that he must take the luggage or not take us, and after a good deal of dilly-dallying he loaded up, and we proceeded. To describe the ride in that Royal mail-coach is impossible; hardly had we left the hotel when our misery commenced. Our seat was a pine board with no back to support you, and nothing to hold on to as you were pitched from side to side. Now when we descend a hill there is a tendency to pitch forward, and again a sudden ascent impels you to turn a back-somersault. Walking was far preferable to riding in such a conveyance, especially as the horses could not move at a faster gait than a walk.

We soon overtook two wagons carrying the lumbermen, as many of them were unable to walk, although some were endeavoring to do so; and they presented a novel sight, too, with handkerchiefs tied about their heads in lieu of the hats they had lost during their drunken revels. The scene that one of the wagons presented was a disgrace to humanity: one of the number was stretched out on his back,—*hors de combat*,—while another was pouring whiskey down his throat, the miserable victim in his stupor not knowing what physic he was taking. We passed this party, glad to get rid of their company. Arrived at Maganetawan at seven P.M., every bone in our bodies sore and tired. Never had such experience in our lives; you pay well sometimes for your sport. That night before retiring to bed sent for a guide, and made arrangements with him.

*Friday, 15th.*—This morning the Governor and myself went fishing on the river, but with no luck. I was so tired last night that I slept soundly, but my companions informed me that though they, too, were tired, sweet sleep visited them not. In its place they passed a restless night, troubled with a multitude of fleas, which gave them no rest. In the afternoon we went out and caught bass and pickerel under the guidance of a gamin called Johnny McCarthy, who was as sharp as a steel-trap, and knew where the fish were to be caught. He was the embryo sportsman. We were obliged to wait this day for the guide, Captain George Ross, who lives three miles from this village, which consists of Scotch settlers and Canadians. There are two small groceries and two inns, at one of which (kept by Clark) we rested.

During the day we sent our traps by stage to the place where we were to camp, seven miles from Clark's. The day was fine, but it rained during the night. I was amused that night to hear the conversation of those assembled at Clark's. This, it seemed, was the rendezvous of the village. During the day a woman had died, and the village carpenter was engaged in making—I will not call it a coffin—a box; it was original. The dead woman had been married a year; the people seemed to mourn her loss, as she was a kind person. It impressed me very much to see the sympathy of the neighbors.

*Saturday, 16th.*—Hired a wagon and started for the camp. After riding a distance we dismounted and took a birch canoe on Canoe Lake, and finally reached our camp. The tent was up and the larder was furnished with a deer, which the guide had killed the day before, besides arranging the camp. We partook to-day, for the first time, of a dinner under a tent in the woods. The change from a set table with all its conveniences to the camp with its improvised accommodations is a decided one, but I think we all enjoyed this dinner, although the Governor wanted a napkin. He was the only one for whom a cup and saucer were procured in Toronto; the rest of the camp and table utensils were of tin. Our camp was delightfully situated about one hundred feet from the lake. We were much pleased with the good taste exhibited by our guide in the selection of the spot. This afternoon we went out hunting, and Dr. W. was the first to bring down a deer, which he killed a short distance from the camp. This afternoon our force was increased by I. Nelson, an old man, and George, his son, a young fellow about twenty. Our number is now six men all told. We have two hounds and two canoes.

Our beds are composed of the tops of firs placed on Mother Earth. The night had its discomforts as well as pleasures; unhappily, we had obtained some blankets from Clark's, and with them was the inevitable flea, which, like the mosquito, gives no rest. We passed a miserable night on account of these pests, but propose to beat them out to-morrow.

*Sunday.*—A day of rest.

*Monday.*—Went fishing on the lake; small trout and chubs are the only fish the lake contains.

*Tuesday.*—The Governor and myself each shot a deer.

*Wednesday.*—Dr. W. went out with the gun and brought in some partridges.

*Thursday.*—This evening we were frightened when

"Tuesday, the Governor and myself each shot a deer."

George set fire to the frying-pan in which he was preparing to cook some fish. His cries of "Water! water!" aroused the whole camp. The next episode was the Governor being nearly frozen to death. He forgot in getting into bed to go between the blankets, and on the dawn of day he became aware of his scanty covering, although we keep up a rousing fire before the tent all night. We have improved our camp, having erected a dining-room near the tent, open on the front and closed in on both sides, with a roof made of pine boughs. Here we have our table, and we are as happy as kings, eating our meals. The Governor insisted that it would be more civilized to eat off a table than off the ground, so we followed his suggestion. The Governor and myself took with us the old man Nelson to visit a beaver-dam, but before we had reached it we got tired and returned; took a gun with us, and killed some partridges,—*a foolish bird.* It flies from the ground and perches on a limb, looking down. If there should be a flock on the tree, the report of a gun will not frighten them away, and, provided you kill the lowest one first, and so on, you may bag the entire lot.

Young George went out to start a deer; did not return till the following day. Says that he lost his way. The opinion of the camp was that he got lazy and slept out in a haystack.

*Thursday, 21st.*—Took a stroll through the woods. In the afternoon a deer was shot; the hinder part was partly eaten by one of the hounds.

*Friday, 22d.*—Broke up camp and went to the head of the lake. The Governor took the stage for Rosseau on his way home. George and his father went home, and we pitched our camp on the shores of the lake. Got milk from Averill's. The captain went in search of another guide. As we were coming down the lake in the canoes, which were loaded to the gunwale, one of the dogs undertook to jump out and come to our canoe, nearly upsetting the one containing the Governor. However, nothing more serious resulted than the shipping of some water and the severe fright to our friend.

Captain Ross now went home, and Dr. W. and myself were alone.

*Saturday*, 23*d*.—The captain came to the camp about ten o'clock, accompanied by Bob Noble, who was to go with us as the second guide. We ate dinner and started up the lake for Maganetawan in a canoe, and reached there in the evening. Camped a little above the falls, near a sawmill. Visited Clark, and was invited by him to rest there that night. Remembering the experience that we had under his roof on our first night at Maganetawan, we replied that he evidently had too many to accommodate already, and only took our supper there. This evening the boy, John McCarthy, begged so hard to accompany us that we finally consented, and a happy boy he was. I think he slept but little that night. He is fourteen years of age, and his whole delight is in fishing. He has never been out on an expedition before.

*Sunday*, 24*th*.—After breakfast at Clark's we started for Burk's Falls, a distance of twenty miles. The morning was fair, but shortly after starting it commenced to rain, and continued all day. We stopped at twelve for lunch and then proceeded,—the captain and I in the little canoe and the doctor and Bob in the larger one. Well provided with rubber outfit, I kept dry, while the others were wet. Arrived safely at Burk's Falls,—named after Burk, who four years ago settled here, and who keeps a store; there is also a post-office and a new hotel building. The enterprise shown by the government is wonderful. Every little settlement has its post-office and regular mail. A steamboat runs from the Falls to Maganetawan every other day. We tried our luck with the fish and caught a nice lot for supper. We camped by the river.

*Monday, 25th.*—Started for Pickerel Lake. Hired Burk's team to take our luggage beyond the first portage. I went with the team; the others by canoe. After the portage was passed the captain and I took one canoe, the doctor and Bob the other. We had not proceeded far when we ran into a snag, and to prevent sinking before we reached the land, I had to hold my hand over the rent in the side of the canoe while Captain Ross paddled us ashore.

With a piece of cloth and an application of warm pitch we were soon afloat again. At noon we took our dinner. The doctor got out his tackle, and in a few moments landed some nice bass and pickerel, which made an appetizing addition to our mid-day meal. He had also two "*rises*" of trout.

Arrived in the evening at Pickerel Lake; went out and caught some bass and pickerel. There is good trout-fishing here. This lake is two miles long. We encamped at the head of it. Four settlers are located on its shores, and live by fishing and hunting as well as by cultivating the ground. Last Saturday our next neighbor, Mossup, killed a black bear about half a mile from our encampment.

It rained nearly all day; too wet to hunt; went trolling in the lake, and caught some very fine bass. In the afternoon tried to start a deer, but failed.

*Wednesday, 27th.*—Equinoctial storm; wet! wet! wet! Went fishing, and caught some fish. Have had no flesh meat since we left Maganetawan. Fish is our principal food. George went out and started a deer, but it took to another lake. It rained all day; very cold; varied by snowing in the evening. The wind was very sharp and cold. Received a visit from Mossup's two sons. Got a supply of potatoes from him. It is remarkable what fine potatoes are raised on this virgin soil.

*Thursday, 28th.*—Still wet and cold. Tried fishing, but the lake was too rough for success. In hopes of providing some partridge for the table we went out with our guns, but the endeavor failed. Had for dinner bouillon, potatoes, carrots, turnips, and onions; splendid appetite. Captain Ross does not know what to do. The doctor has the blues; would like to be home. I went out on the mountain for partridge; no use. In the afternoon went on the lake and caught some fish near the shore, although the lake was covered with white-caps. The doctor is fixing his pants; sewed the pockets up by camp-light.

*Friday, 29th.*—Rained all last night; raining this morning. George started a deer,—a large buck,—but did not get him; he disappeared very mysteriously. A wet day; drooping spirits in camp. Captain George sick: a bloody dysentery; gave him the last of the spirits; he went to Mossup's house. The doctor and Bob are out in the canoe watching for deer. In the afternoon they went out fishing; caught four bass and two pickerel. Made a pond for the fish, but in the morning they were missing, having been taken by the minks.

*Saturday, 30th.*—Wet morning. Went out looking for help; paddled about till ten o'clock, when he got Mossup and his boy to come and help carry the baggage, so that we could go straight on without returning. The captain was unwilling to start, as he said it would rain; but the doctor was determined, and to show it we started on before them, so that they had to follow. It rained a little in the morning,—very little. The doctor and I started with our guns and rods; lost the trail, but kept on our course, and the first thing we met was a high mountain. We faced it, and by hard work, climbing and crawling, we reached the top. A beautiful sight rewarded our efforts: no less than three lakes were to be seen at the foot of the mountain. We also descried our party in a ravine, and built a fire to attract their attention. They saw it, and we hastened to join them. We descended the side of the mountain and found them all right, except that they had decided to camp there for the day. We decided, after partaking of a light meal, to proceed on our way. The account given by the captain of the portage was sufficient to intimidate any one but ourselves. Our word was *Onward!* We were told that we could not make the journey before night, and that when we reached Rock Lake, for which we were bound, there would be no place to pitch our tent. We were resolved, however, to go on, *and we did.* But of all the portages, this beat them all! Through a bog, wet and muddy, over logs, and through bushes, well interlaced, we finally reached our resting-place on Rock Lake. We found that the only place suitable for a camp was on a rocky cliff, about thirty feet above the lake, not more than twenty feet clear on the surface, and little or no wood, as there had been a fire. The lake was alive with fish; the doctor tried them, but they would not bite. Wearied and exhausted, we impatiently awaited the cooking of a pot of beans; and before they were half boiled, so great was our hunger, we attacked the pot.

We had to drive pegs in the crevices of the rock, and in many instances were compelled to put stones as weights on the canvas to keep the tent in place. We slept, however, soundly.

*Sunday, October* 1.—The night was stormy; thunder and lightning with high winds. The guides' tent was blown down on them, but they were so tired that they slept on when they found that their lives were safe, although the manner in which Bob prayed aloud would open the eyes of any saint. The doctor and myself tried to improve on our bed of the previous night by knocking off some of the sharp points of the rocks on which we slept. It was truly the hardest and most uneven that we ever slept on, and we prefer to be excused from a repetition; so, as we had to remain there another night, we tried to make it at least smoother, if not softer. The doctor went out and caught eleven large trout, and as the larder was bare, it is no exaggeration to add that they were very acceptable after yesterday's tramp and our sumptuous (?) supper.

The captain and Bob started back after the rest of the baggage, which they had left where we took lunch, and came into camp about four o'clock P.M. with a beautiful specimen of a large owl that they had shot. The doctor had to provide food for the camp, and brought in a fine lot of trout. We set Bob to work, with an axe, levelling our bed, by cutting out stumps, driving down stones, and raising up others. We had to be careful, for we were limited in space,—liable to fall and break our necks.

It rained all day; the guides were in bad humor.

*Monday, 2d.*—Changed camp to-day. First we had a portage of a quarter of a mile to Mud Lake, followed by a portage of half a mile to Loon Lake, both of which we crossed, and camped between Loon and Grass Lakes. In crossing Loon Lake we trolled and caught some speckled and salmon trout, several weighing from two to three pounds. This is a beautiful lake, and we encamped on a lovely spot. There is about forty rods of ground intervening between the two lakes. We set to work here fixing our camp; the doctor gathering a fine supply of young branches for a bed, whilst I was making a fire to burn the roots and leave the ground nice and dry where we were to sleep. With our delightful situation—plenty of fine fish and an abundance of johnny-cake for supper—we were happy, and slept the sleep of the just.

*Tuesday, 3d.*—Bob went out in quest of a dog that had followed a deer yesterday and had not returned; finally discovered him in the camp of a hunter named Harvey, and returned with him to us. I went out for a stroll and got some partridges. Bob and the captain went after deer in the morning, but were unsuccessful. The doctor started out in the morning in search of partridge, and at four o'clock in the afternoon a furious storm arose. At half-past five we sent Bob out in a canoe across the lake, as we heard the report of the doctor's gun. The thunder and lightning were severe. After a while we made a fire on the border of Loon Lake to direct them home. In the glare of the lightning we saw Bob, in the canoe, shouting with his might and main. He finally reached the shore, though the wind lashed the lake into high waves. Again we heard the report of the doctor's gun; this time the captain took one of the canoes and went in search of the doctor. The storm increased in violence; it was a terrible night. Towards eight o'clock we heard shouting on the lake. It was the captain returning, bringing home my companion,—safe, though wet to the skin. He had built a fire and it had set fire to a decayed tree, which had some time before been struck by the lightning, and for a great distance around the fire lighted up everything, and thus directed the steps of the guide through the darkness to the spot. The doctor had wandered to another lake, and as he thought he was yet on Loon Lake, he lost his way. He had not provided himself with a pocket-compass. It is a serious thing to get lost in the wilds of Canada.

*Wednesday, 4th.*—A fine breakfast,—partridges and splendid trout. We enjoy camp-life very much. Went out deer-hunting, and before noon we had a fine buck hung up, weighing over two hundred pounds. One of the dogs was again lost, and Bob went to hunt him up;

took my breech-loader with him. Scene,—Bob returns, *swearing like a trooper; wet and cold*,—it is now the month of October and ice has already formed,—wants to change his clothing; stands by the camp-fire, dripping wet. In the mean time he shouts to me, "Your gun is lost; it is

"It is a serious thing to get lost in the wilds of Canada."

in the bottom of the lake." He informs me that the dog upset the canoe, and that he was compelled to swim ashore. Went fishing and caught many trout,—as many as we desired. It rained several times to-day. The boy, John, set his trap for mink and caught several. Made a rake to go fishing after my gun that went to the bottom of the lake. Doctor and Bob went to find the lost gun;

the captain and I after deer. We started one, which took to a neighboring lake. Went to this lake, and, the water being clear, we discovered the gun at the bottom. Took a line and hook and brought up the gun, the hook having caught the guard. It seems that there was no dog in the boat, and that Bob was about to fire when the canoe upset; both barrels being cocked, as we discovered when we raised the gun. We joked Bob about the canoe being upset by a dog when there was a man in it. It was worse than sleeping in a haystack. He felt sheepish and considerably "riled"; so much so that he refused point-blank to accompany the doctor in the little canoe. It rained to-day.

*Friday, 6th.*—Started a deer this morning, but after some running it took a direction straight from us, so that we were obliged to give it up. Returned to camp, and after dinner the captain went to try to get a man to help us move, as we have decided to go on to-morrow. We obtained a quantity of potatoes. Several birds were shot, and also a marten. Tried to fish, but they would not "rise."

*Saturday, 7th.*—Broke camp and started to Sand Lake. The portage was three miles long, a good even trail, and we had a man to assist in carrying the luggage. On our way one of the dogs started a deer. The captain, who carried on his shoulders one of the canoes bearing our cooking-utensils and paddles, started on a run two miles from the lake to which we were bound. We proceeded leisurely, shooting partridge as we went along; lost our way, and had to retrace our steps before we got on the right trail. When we approached the border of the lake we found the sand strewn with kettles and pots, and on looking on the lake we beheld the captain driving before him a very fine deer, which the dog had started two miles back. The doctor took the other canoe, and with one of the guns killed the deer. The captain had no weapon with him except the paddle, and this he was unwilling to use on the deer. He kept it swimming until we arrived. We encamped in the midst of a pine grove, the most beautiful spot it was my good fortune to see. There lay the lake in all its natural beauty, backed by beautiful scenery; trees that spring up sixty feet as straight as an arrow before your eye would encounter a single branch. A silence that was solemn. The doctor and myself sat hour after hour gazing on the scene on a moonlight night, as the waters of the lake rippled on, and we exclaimed, "Oh, that a painter worthy of the subject was here!" Here was nature unadorned, in all her primeval beauty. At some distance from us was a house, where we obtained milk and potatoes, which we relished.

*October* 10.—Went to visit W. Tucker, where I dined and procured some bread. It seemed a little strange, after being out in camp, to be within the walls of a house. Had several hunters of the surrounding country to visit us. They were on a hunt; had one deer.

*October* 11.—Went out fishing on the lake in a dugout, and while fishing shot a deer, which I brought to shore, having towed it with the fishing-line. It was slow work bringing it in, as the pesky old dug-out was so easily upset. I astonished the doctor when I informed him that I caught him on the line. We had now two other deer besides mine. This lake is three miles long and one of the most beautiful of lakes.

*October* 12.—Started for home. Crossed the lake, entered the waters of the South River, and paddled with a light heart for the land of the free. We came to Kearney, where there was a store, but no refreshments on hand. Kept on until three o'clock, and then lunched. Started again; found many rapids where we were obliged to walk. Camped at six o'clock; had abundance for dinner,—partridges, venison, and potatoes, no bread. Slept soundly.

*October* 13.—Started early; at the first rapids one of the dogs started a deer; had to wait an hour for the beast. The other canoe went ahead. The canoe leaked badly. Reached Burk's Falls at three and a half P.M. Here we took a steamboat, and after a safe and uneventful journey from this point, we reached home again October 16.

## CHAPTER V.

THE START FOR A GRAND MOOSE- AND DEER-HUNT—SELECTION OF A PHOTOGRAPHER AND THE CHIEF GUIDE—A ROMANTIC WEDDING AND THE HONEYMOON—ARRIVAL AT ROSSEAU VILLAGE—CANADIAN STAGE ROUTE—PROPRIETOR AND DRIVER—OUR OLD FRIEND "CHRIS"—OUR NEW-MADE ACQUAINTANCES—MR. STRUCE, OF BROOKLYN.

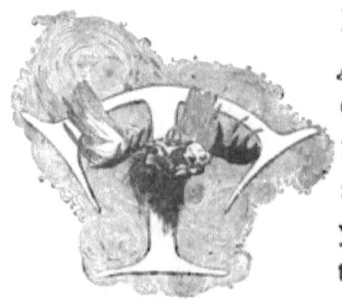

HE necessary preparations for a *grand moose- and deer-hunt* which I commenced in the month of July, 1884, were not completed until the 20th of September in the same year. I had originally anticipated that I would be able to persuade some personal friend to accompany me; but when I informed them that I should probably be away from home at least two months, and that there were certain hardships and privations that were inseparable from moose-stalking, I found no one inclined to become a member of my party. I was therefore placed in a position to organize this expedition on a basis which was strictly in harmony with my own wishes. The great object that I wished to accomplish by this trip was an improvement of my health, inasmuch as I was then suffering from glucosuria, making it necessary for me to take very active exercise, which to a lazy man is commonly felt to be a mean sort of drudgery. I therefore took advantage of my love of the chase, and thereby changed what would otherwise have been an irksome duty into a pleasant pastime. It required but little reflection on my part to discern the advantages that might accrue from the presence of a photographer in my party, since he would enable me to bring away from the wilderness *so many grand scenes* which, otherwise, would be so soon forgotten, even by myself, and never enjoyed by my friends. It was while I was imbued with this idea that I met Anton Mildenberger, an educated gentleman and highly skilled landscape photographer, who very readily consented to become a member of my party. This gentleman possessed in a very high degree those qualities, physical, mental, and social, which are so important in every member of such a hunting-party. The reader will readily perceive that since there is much heavy labor to be performed, especially on the portages, it is very desirable that each member of the party should be able to give some assistance, and it likewise requires physical strength to travel long distances through these unbroken forests. It is equally evident that, prior to engaging a photographer for such an expedition as I was about to start on, his mental and social qualities should be carefully considered. Having given the necessary attention to all these points, I finally determined to employ Mr. Mildenberger.

About the middle of August the terms were arranged, and he was requested to be in readiness for the departure on the 20th of September. I had reached the conclusion, prior to entering on this engagement, that the individual selected for this duty was neither an epicure nor a dude, and therefore I believed that he might be able to content himself in a hunter's camp. This conclusion was, in some measure, based on the fact that I had learned from a thoroughly reliable source that my photographer had served as a private soldier in the German army during the whole of the Franco-Prussian War; and I was then—as I am now—thoroughly convinced that in such a school a *strong character is formed, frivolities forgotten, and manhood developed.* Let the reader study the character of Anton Mildenberger throughout the entire story of this hunt before he declares that the opinion I have just expressed is incorrect.

The selection of the chief guide, although a matter of great importance to any hunting-party, did not in this instance require much thought on my part, as I was thoroughly acquainted with George Ross, who resides at Spence, in the district of Muskoka, province of Ontario, Canada, and with whom the reader has already been made familiar in the preceding pages of this book, especially with his exploits in deer-hunting, etc. These remarkable feats, which have been recorded by my friend and companion in a former hunt in these backwoods, were all familiar to me when I made my arrangements for a third visit to this grand forest. I was likewise aware of the fact that there were then only two competent moose-hunters and guides for all that region which I had determined to enter, and these were Captain George Ross and his brother, Wellington. These brothers were the first white men to penetrate that magnificent forest lying north and northeast of Pickerel Lake and the Lake of the Bays and south of the Ottawa River for the purpose of trapping beaver. This forest still contains many thousand square miles, which are in the same primitive condition as they were a hundred years ago. It was in this great forest that I spent six weeks without meeting a human being, except the members of my own party, or seeing even a trapper's cabin, with the exception of two or three that had been built by the Ross brothers. These brothers had been trapping in that wilderness about fourteen years, and are certain that when they first entered it it did not contain moose nor any trace of those animals. They say that the moose made their appearance here after the prevalence of heavy forest fires which prevailed in the country east of this region, and that this was contemporaneous with the commencement of work on the Canadian Pacific Railroad. I wrote to Captain George Ross, making my engagement with him about the middle of July, 1884; thus early in order that he might prepare the necessary outfit, and likewise construct new birch-bark canoes, and engage an assistant guide, etc. He promptly informed me of his acceptance, and promised to have everything in readiness for us. It was, therefore, with the fullest confidence in the completeness of my arrangements that I took my departure from Jersey City on the evening of the 20th of September, 1884, in company with my photographer.

Nothing of importance transpired until we reached Gravenhurst wharf, on the 22d of September. This occurred at about two P.M., and we went immediately on board of the steamboat "Nippissing," where I met an intelligent gentleman, who informed me that he was one of the first settlers in the vicinity of Rosseau, having settled about thirty years ago in the backwoods, built for himself and wife a small log cabin, and afterwards cut down the forest-trees, changing the wilderness into a farm, on which he reared a family, and where he still continued to reside. He spoke of the sufferings and deprivations endured by himself and other pioneers who first ventured to settle in this cold, rocky wilderness, where they were generally widely separated from each other, and likewise at a great distance from those depots which furnished them with the necessaries of life.

It often became necessary for these pioneers to walk through unbroken forests a distance of forty or sixty miles in order to buy provisions, or even mail a letter, while their only means of transportation, during the season in which the lakes and rivers were not frozen, was the birch-bark canoe; but when these avenues of travel were closed with ice, they were then compelled to perform the labor which, in California and other portions of the United States, is done by pack-mules.

Furthermore, the difficulty which attended this transportation of provisions was not by any means the most serious one with which they had to contend, inasmuch as the amount of cash carried by them into the wilderness was generally very limited, and consequently soon exhausted; a condition which, in some instances, was followed by death from starvation, while in other cases these poor sufferers were compelled to subsist for many weeks on no other food than turnips, eaten without salt or pepper, while at other times a meal was made of birch-buds or seed-potatoes that had been planted some weeks. In order that the reader may understand this dreadful condition of things, he should be informed that the pioneers who first settled on these "Free Grant Lands" *were very poor*, possessing no live-stock of any kind, and in many instances they were even strangers to the American continent,—persons who had been tempted by the offer of lands to leave their homes in Europe, and in many cases, too, these immigrants were entirely ignorant of all agricultural pursuits.

Many of these people became quickly discouraged. Some turned back from the front without even attempting to battle with the cold climate and the discouraging surroundings; some remained there only a few weeks or months, and then left the "Free Grant Lands" *thoroughly discouraged and frequently half famished*. However, there was still another class of these early adventurers who went into this wild wilderness—this land of *beautiful lakes and hills*—possessed of strong hands and strong wills, fully determined to make a home for themselves; and *these have battled bravely; have won, and to them belongs the spoils*. It was to this class that the gentleman whom I met on the boat belonged. He supplied me with much valuable information in regard to the early history of the country about Lakes Muskoka and Rosseau,—a district which is now fairly settled, and where the necessaries, with many of the luxuries, of life are now enjoyed by its inhabitants.

This gentleman, like the *old soldier or sailor* whom we occasionally meet, was delighted with the opportunity that was now offered him to detail to me his struggles and his successes; and I was likewise highly pleased with the information which he imparted. A process similar to that which I have just described, in connection with the lands about these lakes, is now going on in the adjacent territory, although I think the Canadian government is giving more assistance to these struggling pioneers.

Assistance is afforded to the immigrants by the erection of a house at various points along the canoe routes, where provisions are stored, and where the weary traveller is permitted to halt and refresh himself until able once more to move forward. Important assistance is also afforded to these early settlers by the government in the construction of wagon roads, which open up the forest soon after the advance of the pioneers, and the establishment of schools and post-offices wherever demanded by the representative heads of five families. It will thus be observed that the pioneer has no just cause for complaint against the government at the present day.

Having portrayed some of the stern realities of life in these regions, we will now turn to a *more romantic occurrence*, which we are informed was enacted on Lake Rosseau and other neighboring lakes during the summer of 1884. A young gentleman, the son of the pioneer whom I met on the steamboat "Nippissing," had determined to take to himself a wife. He had been employed several years as a clerk in a banking-house at Toronto, and it was in this city that he met the young lady whom he subsequently married. In order that the marriage might be in keeping with the honeymoon, it had been decided that it should be celebrated on a green-clad island in the centre of Lake Rosseau,—the same beautiful sheet of water near which he made his first appearance, as an infant, to the great delight of his father's heart, just twenty-five years prior to this nuptial celebration, which occurred on the twenty-fifth day of June, 1884. Very little preparation had been made on the island, or, in fact, was needed for the proper celebration of this important event, since the underbrush was not, at any point, dense; consequently the assembled guests could pass readily from one part of the beautiful grove to another without that inconvenience that otherwise might have been felt, especially by the ladies in the party. The trees growing on this island consisted principally of five varieties: near the water's edge were seen the graceful tamarack and the beautiful balsam, while rising high above the others and near its centre were observed three great white pines, and these were surrounded by a heavy growth of white and yellow birch-trees.

The appearance of the island has changed very little since the first settlers paddled their birch-bark canoes through the clear waters of Lake Rosseau.

Fire, the great destroyer of the primitive beauty of the surrounding forest, had left this spot untouched, and here stood to-day the same giant trees which forty years ago had served the groom's father as the beacon-guide to his forest home. Great changes during this period had been wrought on the shores of Lake Rosseau; the settlers at various places had made clearings and built for themselves the primitive log cabins, which had, in some cases, passed away, giving place to beautiful frame cottages. Much of the remaining wilderness has been burned over, killing the great forest-trees, which were, however, still standing, speaking to us, like the Egyptian pyramids, of the times that have passed; and these dead trunks without branches are now surrounded by young, living trees, which have sprung up subsequently to these fires. Other changes had already been inaugurated, but not by the sturdy pioneer; these originated with the city denizens, who have selected certain choice spots on which they have erected summer-homes.

We have thus carefully described the island and its surroundings prior to inviting the reader to witness with us the joyful ceremony which was just about to be performed in this romantic spot. The appointed day was at hand; the sun was journeying rapidly towards the western horizon; it was already three o'clock; the hour of four had been fixed for the performance of the ceremony, and our informant had determined to be on the spot in time to witness the arrival of the bride and groom, who, with their city friends, were expected to come on the steamboat, which would land them on the island. The other invited guests, living about the lake, were expected to come in such boats, canoes, etc., as they possessed. Soon after three o'clock there could have been seen approaching the island several small rowboats, a half-dozen canoes, and a single dug-out. Each boat carried several persons, males and females, young and old, attired in their holiday suits: these boats contained the more wealthy class of pioneers with their families. The occupants of the canoes were chiefly males and belonged to the hunting classes. These hunters were for the most part attired in hunting-coats, which were ornamented with much fringe, thus displaying a characteristic of the original inhabitant of these grand forests, and this was further imitated by the *bright colors shown in the various articles of dress, especially in the needle-work that ornamented their moccasins.*

The solitary occupant of the dug-out was a poor immigrant, who had but recently arrived in this country in order to avail himself of the "Free Grant Lands," and likewise settle near his brother, who had preceded him twenty years, having settled on this lake in 1864. It was half-past three o'clock when the steamboat was descried approaching the island from the direction of Toronto. At this moment many of the invited guests residing about the lake had effected a landing. The boats and canoes of these were drawn well on *terra firma*, while there was still a certain number of the small water-craft to be seen on the lake.

The point selected for the landing of the steamboat was well chosen. It was directly in front of a large, flat rock, which extended from the water's edge back several rods into the forest, while its width was about one-third of its length. The upper surface of this rock did not rise at any point materially above the surface of the surrounding earth, while the water in front of it was now more than six feet deep, enabling the steamer to approach, run out its ordinary gang-plank, and deliver its passengers without the slightest danger, having been previously made fast by means of ropes to two balsam-trees which were standing in convenient positions. This steamboat had been the principal object of attention by all parties assembled on the island, from the moment when she was first sighted in the distance until they greeted her arrival at this point. Especially had the group seated on her upper forward deck been the object of attention. This party was composed of an equal number of neatly-clad males and females, who had seated themselves in chairs, that had been arranged more or less regularly around the central figures, —the bride and groom.

This company was composed mainly of the bride's relatives who resided in the vicinity of Toronto. The bride was, this day, the most important personage in the whole party, and therefore entitled to a brief description at our hands, although our informant was not able to give us all the information that we desired, especially that which related to her trousseau, and therefore our readers must pardon the omission of much which would certainly serve to embellish this part of our story. The bride had just attained her twentieth birthday, and had received, through the careful attention of her parents, a sound education. It had been their strongly-cherished desire to prepare her for the stern duties of life rather than to give her a mere smattering of those branches of learning that are merely ornamental, and often learned only to be forgotten a few months after leaving the recitation-room. She had, therefore, been thoroughly trained by her mother in the management of household affairs, even without neglecting the highly-important lessons in domestic economy. She likewise possessed a thorough English education, having shown in school a great aptness for mathematical studies, in which she particularly excelled.

In personal appearance she was comely without being

a remarkable beauty. She had been a great favorite with the gentlemen, but no man lived who could truthfully assert that she had ever flirted. Her figure was symmetrical and her movements graceful. She stood about five feet and ten inches, attired as she was on the day that she was married. She belonged to that class of beauties commonly designated as brunettes, having a dark complexion, black hair, brown eyes, and a well-rounded face. Her forehead was moderately high and rather broad. The eyes were of medium size, full, and when in repose wore a kindly expression, but were capable, under excitement, of expressing the deepest love or the most intense hatred. The nose was rather long, but shapely; mouth only of medium size; chin well rounded and not too prominent. It will not now surprise the reader when informed that this lady's countenance, in repose, seemed only moderately attractive, but when lighted up with strong excitement it became divinely expressive. The groom, who now sat at her side, was tall and rather slender, his figure erect, bearing dignified, movements slightly awkward, while the expression of his countenance wanted a little in that firmness and force which characterized the bride's. He was fully six feet in height, having a light complexion, light-brown hair, light-blue eyes, which were slightly sunken, thin face, with thin straggling side-whiskers, a small nose, moderately large mouth, and a slightly-receding chin and forehead. We have now given the reader as much of the personality of the bride and groom as will amply suffice for this occasion. In the matter of dress, we can only say that the groom wore a soft felt hat, and that not a single silk hat was to be seen in the whole party. The ladies were neatly attired for the occasion, but silk and satin dresses were conspicuous only by their entire absence. Bright-colored ribbons and good cheer prevailed among the assembled females. Let us now return to the landing of the guests whom we have carefully surveyed on the steamer's deck. The moment this vessel had been made fast the party seated on the upper deck arose and descended to the gang-plank, over which they passed, the ladies resting gracefully on the arms of their escorts, the bride and groom being the third couple to land. The party passed forward over the smooth but gradually ascending surface of the rock, which has already been described, in the same order they had left the steamer, until they were hidden in the grove. The moment they stepped from this rock they found the earth covered with a thick layer of beautiful moss, extending in every direction about them for many rods, while in front there had been arranged an elegant arch, formed by entwining the branches of two neighboring trees, and this bower had been handsomely decorated with wild flowers, conspicuous among which were the wild roses that abound along the shores of this lake. When the first couple reached this spot they halted, the lady dropped the arm of her escort and passed to the right, the gentleman passing to the left; then each faced about towards the landing-place, thus making room for the others who formed under the beautiful arch. The bride and groom were the third couple to take their place in nature's bower, and when they had faced towards the lake there were now seen standing to the right of the bride three fair ladies, while the groom was supported on his left by the same number of gentlemen. The invited guests now faced the bride and groom. At this moment there appeared before them an old gentleman wearing the official robes of an Episcopal clergyman, holding in his hand a book. The ceremony is quickly performed, congratulations are in order; many voices are heard on every side, but there was no formal wedding reception. Baskets are brought forward,— their contents quickly arranged on the linen which had been spread for this purpose on the green moss, and all this joyous party now partake of the refreshments, giving to the assemblage the appearance of a grand picnic in nature's grandest forest. All things must end, and so did this grand festival. Night was approaching, and the invited guests must return; but we must look a little further after the newly-wedded couple. Before the steamer took her departure from the island the deck-hands had been observed to bring on shore a beautiful Peterborough canoe, and others soon followed who carried two leather valises, two camp-stools, and several bundles. All these various articles had been temporarily deposited on the rock near the water's edge.

The remnants of the refreshments having been gathered up and replaced in the baskets, a party of men are seen to go down to the canoe, seize hold of the bundles, valises, camp-stools, etc., and bring them forward to the arch, beneath which was quickly erected a new, beautiful, and commodious tent. A balsam bed was quickly made within it, and the other household goods properly arranged. The invited guests soon take their leave of the newly-wedded pair; the steamer takes its departure from the rock, where it had remained in waiting for the passengers. The bride and groom have come to the water's edge to receive the parting salutes of their friends; the row-boats, canoes, and the dug-out have all withdrawn from the island, and the wedded pair have retired from the lake-shore to the bridal bower, where they remained the sole occupants of this island for about forty-eight hours. They then started on an extended and novel wedding-tour, which lasted some six weeks, during which period they travelled more than one thousand miles on these mountain lakes. The Peterborough canoe, which has already been mentioned, served as the vehicle for their journeyings, and the handsome tent which was erected on the island soon after the performance of the marriage ceremony was their bridal-chamber. They spent only a small portion of their honeymoon on Lake Rosseau, but passed from one mountain lake to another, the husband transporting the canoe and other luggage on the portages, while the wife walked at his side, or more frequently followed behind him in true Indian style. Thus they journeyed from lake to lake, visiting the pioneer villages situated on these beautiful bodies of water for the purpose of purchasing such supplies as their frugal mode of life required. Here, on the lakes of this wild mountain country, in the bright summer months of June and July, they continued to bask in sunshine and love, undisturbed by the rude and unsympathetic crowds that are often met with on the ordinary highways of travel.

We find it impossible, while contemplating the wander-

A wedding in the wilderness.

ings of the newly-wedded pair in this wild and romantic region, to refrain from following with our imagination the ancient Huron and his new-made wife. If we go back only a few decades in the history of this country we find it in the possession of a mighty tribe of Indians,—the Hurons, who were ruthlessly destroyed by their implacable enemy, the Iroquois.

However, if we believe the history which has been transmitted to us, we find very little in the relation of these scenes that would be pleasing to the reader in this connection. "Female life among the Hurons had no bright side. It was a youth of license, an age of drudgery." It must, therefore, be apparent to any one that a comparison here would be odious, and consequently we will now bid adieu to the newly-wedded pair. In the contemplation of that which we have written on this subject, the inquiry forces itself upon us, Why have the names of these interesting persons been omitted while other details have been given? In reply to this inquiry the author would say that it was the father of the groom who gave him most of the points that have been here interwoven in this narrative, and therefore he withholds the names by request of his informant. Furthermore, it will be observed that this story, involving a marriage and a wedding-tour, is only a wild flower, plucked from our pathway through the wilderness, presented to the reader for momentary gratification; but it forms no essential part of the general character of this book. Pardon, therefore, our digression, and go with us to the Mountain House in the village of Rosseau, where we arrived about six o'clock on the evening of the 22d of September.

It was in the office of this hotel that I first observed Mr. Struce, of Brooklyn, New York, whom I recognized as a sportsman by his dress, and the fact that he was carrying a gun. This gentleman afterwards became a member of our party, and remained with us a few days while we were encamped on Lake Ahmic, near Maganetawan village. The hotel at which we were stopping, now the only one at this point, was the resort of all the loungers of the village as well as travellers.

The evening meal was served in the dining-room soon after our arrival, and there seemed to be about thirty guests in the hotel.

Experience had already taught me that it is very difficult to advance from this point into the forest if you are burdened with more than ten or twelve pounds of luggage, and consequently at an early hour in the evening I began to make inquiry in regard to a conveyance to take us to Maganetawan village, situated about thirty-seven miles from this place.

I learned at the hotel-office that a stage, now owned and driven by a Mr. Bess, would leave for Maganetawan the next morning, arriving at its destination some time in the evening of the same day. The proprietor of this line was soon pointed out to me, and in answer to my question, "Can you take us to Maganetawan to-morrow?" he inquired, "How much baggage have you?" I informed him that we had about one hundred and fifty pounds. He immediately replied, "I cannot take your baggage to-morrow; but I can take you and your companion, and will deliver your baggage for you at Maganetawan village within one week, at an extra charge of six dollars." The regular stage fare for a passenger between these points is a dollar and fifty cents, while for four times that amount the accommodating stage-owner was willing to transport for us, provided we allowed him one week in which to do the work, one hundred and fifty pounds of baggage. I urged this stage-driver very strongly to provide some means by which our baggage would reach Maganetawan the next day; was willing to give him the additional six dollars, but he positively refused. In fact, he showed no disposition to aid us in our efforts, and said that he already had as many passengers, who had engaged seats in his stage, as he could conveniently carry. This disinclination to accommodate travellers seemed to me very strange and entirely incomprehensible; but a subsequent investigation supplied me with a partial explanation. This man, Bess, through political influence, had secured the contract to carry the mail on that line, but inasmuch as he was entirely wanting in enterprise, he had neglected to provide for the accommodation of the travelling public. The explanation of how he could afford to carry passengers over the line for one dollar and fifty cents, while he demanded four times as much for transporting the same weight in baggage, is possibly found in the fact that the accommodations for passengers within his stage are so bad that all passengers are compelled, in self-interest, to walk at least three-fourths of the whole distance. It will, therefore, be observed that the one dollar and fifty cents paid by a passenger really entitles him to ride only about nine miles on the Queen's highway in Bess's stage. This stage was owned and managed, in the autumn of 1880, by a good-natured and accommodating German, familiarly called "Chris," of whom I shall have something to say hereafter. My attempt to negotiate for the transportation of my party and our luggage with Mr. Bess ended in a failure. Further inquiry at the hotel-office afforded nothing satisfactory. It is true I learned that there was no one living in the village, owning horses, who would be willing to take us to our destination. This was not in the least encouraging. I was determined, however, to go forward on the following day if it were possible. I made inquiry in regard to the feasibility of obtaining a team or transportation from some farmer living in the vicinity. The first objection made to this plan by the bystanders was, "You will find it impossible to get a messenger to go into the country among the farmers to-night; it is too late," although it was not yet ten o'clock. I had already been more than two hours engaged in my efforts to secure transportation, but without success. At this moment I discovered Chris, and immediately approached him, when he extended his hand and asked if I was out on another hunting expedition. I answered in the affirmative, and then made known to him my pressing wants. He said, "I am here with my old team, but my wagon is already loaded with merchandise for Maganetawan, some portions of which is in urgent demand." I saw that here was my only chance. Chris would like very much to oblige me; it was not easy for him to say "no." He told me that within a few weeks he had been very unfortunate,—his dwelling-house had been burned, with all his household furniture; that a portion of the load on his wagon at the present time was window-glass intended for the new domicile that he was now erecting. I inquired, "What will you charge to take us with our luggage to Maganetawan to-morrow?" He replied, "It is worth about six dollars, but I don't think I can do it to-morrow." I observed that his manner was somewhat hesitating. Chris was not entirely satisfied with himself and his answer. I said to him, "Chris, remove your load and take us to Maganetawan to-morrow, and I will give you twelve dollars for the job." A smile came over his face; it was evident that I had won. In a few moments he said, "The load shall come off my wagon and you shall be in Maganetawan to-morrow night. What hour do you wish to start?" I said, "You may suit yourself in that matter." He replied, "All right; let us get away from here very early. I will call you at four o'clock."

It was about fifteen minutes after four when Chris knocked at my door the next morning. I was then already dressed, and so was the photographer, who had occupied the room with me during the night. We followed Chris down-stairs and there found Mr. Struce, who was at this moment standing with his gun in hand ready to accompany us. We had not yet spoken together; he had learned that Chris was engaged to take myself and the artist to Maganetawan, and had determined to accompany us. He had already made an arrangement with Chris, and was now ready to start, instead of waiting for the Bess stage until a late hour. He greeted us pleasantly when we came into his presence that morning, saying, "Good-morning, gentlemen. I have determined to travel with you to-day, unless you have some objection." I promptly assured him that we should be very happy to have his company, especially as I recognized him as a brother sportsman. Here began a very pleasant acquaintance.

## CHAPTER VI.

OUR DEPARTURE FROM ROSSEAU—A CHARMING MORNING AND A HEALTHFUL WALK—CAMPED NEAR SPENCE—INCIDENTS WHICH OCCURRED THERE—JOINED BY OUR GUIDES—CAMPED ON BIRCH ISLAND—CAMP-LIFE ON AHMIC LAKE—STRUCE STARTS FOR HOME—THE BALANCE OF THE PARTY OFF ON A LONG TRAMP—THE BEAVER'S TRYSTING-PLACES—THE PHOTOGRAPHER'S SPORT NEAR BURK'S FALLS—PLODDING THROUGH WOODS AFTER DARK—THE YOUTHFUL DRIVER—ARRIVAL AT SPHYNX SHOOT.

IT was nearly five o'clock on the morning of the 23d of September when our party took their departure from Rosseau. The darkness of night still enshrouded the earth; the air was cold and chilly, while the ground was covered with a heavy frost. Chris's old gray horses, which are now at least twenty-one years of age, moved forward just as well as they did four years ago when I rode behind them over the same route. The morning is so chilly that Chris, Struce, and Mildenberger prefer to walk rather than ride in this wagon, which is not supplied with springs, over the rocky mountain road. I have, therefore, at the request of Chris, mounted the driver's seat, wrapped myself in the horse-blankets, seized the reins and whip, and am thus duly installed in this new position.

The photographer and Mr. Struce very soon disappeared in the darkness after leaving the hotel, but Chris remained near the team to give me such instruction as was needed to pass the team safely over this road. The cold was so severe and the road so rough that, having ridden about three miles, I called on Chris to resume the charge of his team, while I was now ready to follow the example of my companions. The gray dawn of the morning had made its appearance in place of the dim starlight that prevailed at the time we started from Rosseau. Having transferred the reins to Chris I descended from the driver's seat, passed to the front of the team, and started forward at a lively pace, determined to quickly overtake Struce and Mildenberger.

It was probably about half an hour before I caught sight of my companions, who were still about a mile ahead of me, and moving forward at good speed, while the sun was now shining brightly, lighting up the hill-tops, causing the frozen drops of water, which were clinging to the branches of leafless trees, to sparkle with the resplendent beauty of pure diamonds in a bright gas-light. The grandeur of this scene afforded me the purest joy. I inhaled this mountain air—loaded with ozone—as the hungry man partakes of the choicest viands. The rapid step at which I was moving forward caused me to expel, in the first part of my journey, **the old** residuary air with which the lungs of every sedentary **person are** more or less filled, thereby enabling me to seize and appropriate a very large quantity **of** this grand atmospheric stimulant, which **now** caused the blood **to** course rapidly through **every part** of the body, producing **a joyous thrill** in **every fibre.**

In this mental and physical condition it was a pleasure

to move rapidly forward. The reader will not, therefore, be surprised when informed that I soon found myself in the company of my companions, who had taken the lead immediately after our departure from the hotel at Rosseau. We now journeyed on together, and reached the "Ten-Mile Lake Hotel" before eight o'clock. Here we ordered breakfast, which was to be served as soon as Chris should arrive with his team and our baggage. My companions had walked this morning, without food or stimulants, except that supplied by an invigorating atmosphere, ten miles. I had walked seven and did not feel fatigued. It was more than an hour after our arrival here before Chris came up with his team.

The long journey had fully prepared us to enjoy the breakfast, which consisted, principally, of delicious venison, pure country butter, home-made bread, coffee, and wild honey. I am sure that our entire party, this morning, thought our breakfast good enough for a king.

Every article of food placed before us was of excellent quality, and the serving could not have been improved. We complimented the hostess on her excellent table; she thanked us kindly, and, having probably learned that we hailed from the United States, then inquired if any one in our party was acquainted in New Hampshire, which, she now informed us, was her native place. We were compelled to answer her inquiry in the negative, but she now volunteered the information that she had only lived in Canada since her marriage.

We had already spent at this wayside hotel more than two hours; the sun was still shining brightly, but it was necessary for us to go forward in order that we might reach the end of our journey this day before nightfall. We were now about twenty-seven miles from Maganetawan, and nearly twenty-one from Spence, the home of Captain George Ross, whom I had engaged as our chief guide. It is not yet certain whether we shall remain tonight at Spence or go on to Maganetawan, inasmuch as I have not consulted with the captain in regard to our future movements. The team plodded steadily along the mountain-road to-day. Neither Mr. Struce nor Mildenberger have ridden in the wagon. They started on foot and so continue to journey on.

It was about three o'clock when we arrived at Spence, a small hamlet, consisting of a wayside hotel, post-office, and about half a dozen log cabins. We halted at the hotel for our dinner, while Chris took this opportunity to feed his team. Immediately after our arrival I succeeded in finding a messenger, whom I sent to Captain Ross's residence, which is situated about one-half mile from the hotel, with instructions to bring him to me. The messenger returned, after an absence of about forty minutes, accompanied by a young man, who informed me that the captain was away from home, engaged in a deer-hunt, but would certainly return within a few hours, as he was expecting the arrival of my party on the following day. After a brief consultation with the young man, who informed me that he was now staying at the captain's house, and had received instructions prior to the captain's departure that should we arrive during his absence he—the young man —was to make us comfortable, I determined to halt at this place, or near it, and await the return of our guide. The dinner being finished we again started forward, after having spent about an hour and a half at the hotel. We camped this night in the woods near the roadside, about one mile from the hotel at Spence where we had dined, and about five miles from the village of Maganetawan, while our tent was now standing within forty rods of Ahmic Lake.

The young man who has already been mentioned as having reported to me on the return of the messenger whom I had sent for the captain, after my arrival at Spence, was now with us. He had brought with him from the captain's cabin an axe, which is so necessary in a hunter's camp. Five minutes after our arrival on the ground where we had determined to camp, it was plainly evident to me that my new-made friend was not a novice at this sort of work. He knew exactly what was necessary to be done, and was not slow in giving assistance. It required but a few minutes to erect our tent, and make all the needed preparations for the night; but this had scarcely been completed when the rain commenced to fall, although the sky had been cloudless when we arrived at the hotel in Spence. The young man proposed to bring us our suppers from the captain's cabin, but this was deemed unnecessary by the whole party, inasmuch as we had partaken of our dinner at a late hour.

The first night under the canvas was spent very comfortably, while a bright fire burned in front of our open tent until long after midnight. Notwithstanding the fact that a heavy rain-storm had set in, we remained perfectly dry and serenely happy.

*September* 24.—The rain is still falling. The young man who was instructed by the captain to look after us during his absence was in camp with our breakfast soon after seven o'clock this morning. He came provided with the necessary cooking utensils to serve it hot. Having completed our breakfast, the photographer took up my Ballard rifle and asked the young man to accompany him to the lake. He had not been absent from the tent five minutes when I heard the report of the gun; other shots followed this; seven had soon been fired. There was a lapse of probably about three minutes after the last report was heard when Mildenberger made his appearance before the tent asking for a shot-gun, *saying at the same time, excitedly, " I have just fired five shots at a partridge sitting on a tree, and the young man has fired two; the bird has not moved, and I don't believe she knows that she is wanted."* It has previously been mentioned that Mildenberger had served in the artillery with the German army during the Franco-Prussian war, but these shots failed to convince us that he was skilled in the use of the rifle. In fact, other observations forced the conclusion that he had not, prior to this, been accustomed to the use of even a shot-gun. He proved, however, to be a very apt scholar in these matters, and before he left the woods he was quite an expert in the use of both the shot-gun and rifle. I saw him with the shot-gun handsomely drop birds on the wing, while with the rifle he could occasionally knock off a partridge's head without injuring its body. At the particular time when he required a shot-gun to compel the partridge to recognize that she was wanted, the bird—it is thought—became impatient, since Mildenberger has not yet succeeded in finding her, although he has made long and diligent search.

The phrase, "I don't believe she knows that she is wanted," became one of very common use in our party, and was applied on all occasions when the game remained uninjured after a shot was fired.

The rain continued to fall until about ten o'clock, when the clouds showed some signs of breaking, and the sun occasionally peeped out through an open space, although there was very little clear sky visible during the day. Struce and Mildenberger succeeded in taking some fine bass in Ahmic Lake during the afternoon. I took a stroll through the wood, accompanied by two cocker-spaniels, which are to take part with us in this campaign. I was not fortunate in finding game: saw only a single bird.

Captain Ross and his nephew made their appearance in our camp before sunset. The captain greeted me pleasantly. We had not met during the preceding four years, and as he now stood before me he appeared the same as when I parted with him at Spence, in the autumn of 1880, after we had finished that hunt.

He now introduced us to his nephew, George Ross, and informed me that he had engaged this man to accompany us as a guide. Struce and Mildenberger were made acquainted with these men who were to become members of our party. It had also been previously agreed between Struce and myself that an additional guide would be at least desirable as long as Mr. Struce remained in our party. I therefore made inquiry of the captain about his brother, Wellington, with whom I was somewhat acquainted, know-

"I don't believe she knows that she is wanted."

ing that no better guide could be found in the region of Maganetawan. He replied, "I think Wellington will be able to be with us after a few days."

The captain, with the assistance of his nephew, made all the necessary arrangements for the night. Wood was provided, supper prepared, and the captain's tent put up. In the mean time it has been arranged that a deer-hunt shall take place to-morrow on Ahmic Lake. The guides will now remain constantly with us in camp; this will be a marked improvement, and will add much to our happiness and comfort.

The party, as now arranged, consists of five persons, and we are provided with five dogs,—two of them intended to be employed in deer-hunting, while three are cocker-spaniels, used only in bird-shooting. The following morning the sport commenced at an early hour, and we were back in our camp before eleven o'clock. Struce and myself, with the guides, had hunted deer, while Mildenberger had started out in search of ruffed grouse.

The sport opened this morning fairly well. Struce shot a fawn, Mildenberger killed four partridges, and I took some bass while on the way to the point, where I was stationed by the captain to watch for deer.

A good dinner was served for us by our guides on our return to camp. We had brought into camp some delicacies, and likewise tin plates, tin cups, etc.; consequently our table and culinary department were quickly placed on a sound basis. The camp which we had formed by the wayside, immediately after our arrival, was thought to be no longer desirable, and consequently our guides moved our quarters, on the afternoon of September 25, to Birch Island, which is situated in Lake Ahmic.

The photographer was at the same time engaged in taking some views on this lake, while I was absent searching for ruffed grouse. We were joined in the evening by Wellington Ross, who now becomes a member of our party. The sport went on, from day to day, in about the same manner as has been already detailed. The evenings were passed very pleasantly before the camp-fire; the captain and his brother, although very modest men, have had a large experience in hunting and trapping, and they narrate this experience in a quaint and quiet way, after we finally succeed in getting them started.

Wellington has spent a few years on the Pacific coast, and describes the game and the methods of hunting in that region, as well as the nature of the country, the timber-growths, etc. Our friend Struce, who classes himself among the amateur sportsmen of the United States, has certainly sufficient experience to enable him, in camp, to add his full quota to the enjoyment of a party of hunters. *He tells a bear story well, although he does not even claim to have hunted bruin.* The captain has killed several bears, but these animals with which he came in contact and slaughtered were, apparently, very well behaved, and died without making any unusual fuss about it.

Thus day after day was passed in hunting and fishing and social intercourse around the camp-fire; but at last our friend Struce decided that he could remain no longer with us, and that the next day he must take his departure for Brooklyn. It had been intended by the whole party that our photographer should take a camp picture prior to this separation. That design, however, was frustrated by a pouring rain that continued during the whole day prior to his departure, September 29. This morning was clear and bright. We were up and stirring before it was fairly light. Having breakfasted, Captain Ross and Struce started for Spence, where the latter expected to meet the stage from Maganetawan, which was to take him to Rosseau on his way home. The captain's deer-dogs have not been in camp for the past twenty-four hours. I speak of the captain's deer-*dogs* instead of employing the word *hounds*, for the reason that there is not a drop of hound blood in their veins. These dogs are really mongrels, although I presume the collie breed predominates. The collie breed is highly praised by all the backwoodsmen with whom I have come in contact in Canada. He is praised as a valuable house-dog, an excellent dog with cattle, and when trained to run deer some claim to think him even superior to the hound.

The captain's dogs were certainly very good animals. When placed on a deer's track they seldom failed to run him to water, but the one fault which I desire here to mention with regard to this entire breed of dogs is, that when used in hunting deer they give very little "tongue." This *one defect* in the dog deprives the sportsman of the *excitement and pleasure* which he would otherwise feel in listening to the voice of the running hound. To my ear there are few sounds more charming. I listen eagerly to this music in order to determine the approach of the deer, and the hound's loud voice on a cool, frosty morning, although it may be only faintly heard, serves to make the blood course more rapidly through my veins, while at the same time it cheers my spirits and warms my body. Give me, therefore, the musical hound in deer-hunting, instead of the best collie ever imported from old Scotland.

The captain has gone in search of his pets. Wellington and George Ross are packing the camp equipage this morning, that we may be off for Burk's Falls. An acquaintance of the guides, whom they address as "Isaacs," has made his appearance in our camp. He is out searching for a lost dog. He is urged by the guides to take a hand in our moving, and finally consents. Therefore a portion of luggage was placed in his bateau for transportation to Maganetawan, which we reached about half-past nine o'clock, having travelled this morning in our canoe about three miles.

These canoes and our luggage were placed on the little river steamer "Pioneer," which is to take us up the Maganetawan River to Burk's Falls, distant from this village about thirty-five miles.

The captain made his appearance soon after our luggage had been loaded on the little steamer, but he had not succeeded in finding his lost dogs. He is, therefore, compelled to remain behind and make further search for the animals, which are indispensable in hunting deer at this season of the year, when the trees are still covered with leaves. The loss of deer-hounds or other dogs that are employed in deer-hunting is not an infrequent occurrence, and commonly happens by the dogs continuing to follow a deer to some distant lake. The reader will readily perceive by what has already been said that the deer does not always come to the exact spot at which the sportsman is stationed, or even to the lake at which he is wanted.

Few dogs possess sufficient sagacity to return on their own trail and thus reach their master. I have seen only a single animal that would uniformly follow out this course. That dog, an animal called "Fan," was the property of Dr. Pokorney, and has already been described in this book.

When the captain reached us, he soon learned that his brother had gone to his house in the village of Maganetawan, and he promptly started to find him, in order that Wellington might accompany us in his (the captain's) place. This arrangement may last only a few days, or it may be a week before the captain's search will be rewarded by finding his lost pets. We left Maganetawan about eleven o'clock in the morning, and reached Burk's Falls before four o'clock P.M.

The scenery along this river is certainly very picturesque. The banks are covered with heavy forest-trees, and there are aquatic plants and bushes growing in the shallow water along the shore. The amount of clearing along the banks of this river, seen from the decks of our little steamer, was very limited in the autumn of 1884. Captain Ross, when descending the Maganetawan in company with the author, in 1880, pointed out to us the very spot where several years ago he saw his first moose. He gave us a clear description of the animal, and did not seem well pleased with himself because he had failed to kill the monster with a single charge of buckshot, which he gave him with his compliments, this being the best he could do under the circumstances.

It was during this same trip down the river that the captain greatly interested me by the description which he gave of the beaver "trysting-places." The captain is certainly a matter-of-fact man, possessed of no romantic ideas, and yet the statements which he made on this occasion may seem to savor strongly of fiction, although I am fully convinced that he believes in the beaver "trysting-place," and in all the details that he has given pertaining to the same, including even the acting of the animals. The narrator commenced by saying that many years ago, while travelling through these woods, he discovered a mound that had been recently raised by the heaping up of the soft earth, the measurements of the same being about two feet in diameter and about six inches in height, while it was almost circular in outline. This mound bore the positive impress of the animal by which it had been reared, and this serves as the beaver's "trysting-place."

In order that we might understand the nature and necessity of the trysting-places, the captain made the following statement: "It is chiefly in winter that the beavers congregate, and then only a single family occupies the same lodge or house, although there may be several families living within the waters raised by the dam that has been erected by their united efforts. The family may consist of a single adult, male and female, or they may have with them two, four, six, or eight of their own offspring, which have not yet fully matured. When, however, these young beavers are fully grown, they go forth from the parental roof in search of a partner, with the intention of establishing a new home. It also frequently happens that the family circle has been impaired through the agency of the hunter or trapper,—that the father or mother has been trapped or killed. Under these circumstances the survivor takes upon himself, or herself, the entire charge of the family. Sooner or later, however, the young will mature and go forth in search of mates, while the adult must again start on this journey. It is a well-recognized fact that single beavers are sometimes found which live apart from all others of their species. There are wanderers which, during the summer months, are travelling about, bent on the accomplishment of the object of their lives,—impelled by a God-given power,—seeking a companion in order to make a home and rear a family. Furthermore, they are strictly *monogamic* in their habits, and while the first partner survives none other is permitted to enter the family circle. It is," said the captain, "for the accomplishment of this object that the mounds are erected by the lonely traveller; and it is on these mounds that they declare to the opposite sex their desire to effect a union by depositing here a small quantity of castoreum, which is generated in two glandular pouches situated near the organs of reproduction, and the odor of which sufficiently differs in the sexes to be instantly recognized by these keen-scented animals at long distances. Therefore the wanderer, without regard to sex, is enabled to raise a mound, deposit thereon the lover's proclamation, which will be scented and understood of the opposite sex within a large radius, while the suitor, seeking companionship, lingers near the 'trysting-place' until the inamorata approaches in answer to the call."

If the captain is correct in the opinion which he has expressed on this subject, may we not find in his theory a full explanation of the fact that the castoreum, which trappers have long been accustomed to employ as a bait on the trap to lure the poor beaver to death, depends solely on this magical power?

I am aware of the fact that the mounds mentioned by Captain Ross have not been generally recognized by our backwoodsmen, but this does not materially impair the force of his statement. The captain does not claim that they are very numerous, but says that he has seen several such mounds in the Canadian wilderness.

Immediately after the arrival of the steamer at Burk's Falls my party proceeded to make such purchases as were thought necessary. A store of provisions was laid in sufficient to last the party eight weeks, with such additions as were expected to be obtained by the use of the rod and gun. These purchases were made with very little loss of time.

We now hired of the merchant from whom we purchased our supplies a horse and wagon to take our canoes and other luggage up the north branch of the Maganetawan River, to a point just above Sphynx Falls. This portage was made necessary by the fact that the river was filled with mill-logs up to the falls mentioned, and, consequently, could not be traversed by our canoes. It may be well to state in passing that Burk's Falls probably possesses more than ordinary attractions for business men and others seeking new homes in this region. It is the natural terminus of steamboat navigation on the Maganetawan River, and there is at this point a very great amount of water-power which may be easily made available for manufacturing purposes. In addition to all this, the country about here is heavily timbered, and the river enables the lumberman to bring the logs here more cheaply than they can be delivered at any other point where they would possess the same value. In other words, nature points to this spot as the most desirable one in this entire district for the conversion of raw material into manufactured products.

It was about five o'clock when the wagon, loaded with our canoes and other luggage, was ready to start from Burk's Falls for Sphynx Shoot, which is distant from the former place about three miles. The driver of the wagon, a boy about twelve years of age, had stood patiently by the horse watching the guides while they loaded our baggage. The moment this work was completed he mounted the wagon, found a seat on some of our luggage, and began to urge his horse forward. The horse was not much younger than the boy, but both performed their share of the work satisfactorily, while at the start Wellington and George Ross followed the wagon closely to prevent damage being done to our luggage. The country through which this rough road passes is made up of rocky hills and low marshy ground, but at this time, owing to the fact that it was unusually dry, we were enabled to traverse it quite satisfactorily until the darkness of night began to gather about us.

Mr. Mildenberger, the photographer, had started out

slightly in advance of the wagon, accompanied by "Ponto," in search of ruffed grouse. He had not been out ten minutes when the barking of "Ponto" was heard, and within the next five minutes he had fired two shots. A few minutes later he returned to the road with "Ponto" at his heels. The author was walking some distance in advance of the wagon which was loaded with our baggage, and was therefore, at this moment, in full view of our amateur sportsman, who drew proudly from his pockets two fine birds which he had just shot, having killed them with the shot-gun, since he had not become sufficiently expert in the use of the rifle to be able to convince a ruffed grouse that he "was wanted" when the gun was fired.

The photographer now sent "Ponto" once more into the woods. Soon after a loud and lively barking was heard, and our amateur sportsman was again quickly lost to our sight; had gone again into the dense woods that form the boundary on either side of the rough country road throughout the greater part of the whole distance between Burk's Falls and Pickerel Lake. The sound of his gun was again heard; the dog soon after this rushed once more across our front, but quickly returned to a spot not far distant from where the last shot was fired. In a few moments the sound of another shot resounded throughout the forest; the photographer is already flushed with victory. Shot after shot is heard. Darkness was approaching and he was soon compelled to return from the woods, because it was so dark that he could no longer see the game; but he was not satisfied, although he had killed six beautiful birds in somewhat less than an hour. He complained that darkness had so soon cut short his sport.

He was now compelled to walk in the centre of the road, by the side of the author. Onward they trudged while the twilight was rapidly disappearing. The rumbling sounds of the wagon were occasionally heard in our rear, while the guides were aiding our youthful driver. The stars had become visible, but the moon had not condescended to make her appearance.

Large trees stood in close proximity to the wagon-path. Some had fallen across it. The woodman's axe had in some cases cut its way through the trunk of the fallen giant of the forest, while the hardy son of toil had rolled the obstruction to one side to allow a vehicle to pass. In other instances the fallen trunk, being somewhat smaller, had not been removed, and the driver was compelled to pass over it, or if the condition of the ground at this point was favorable, a road would be made around the obstruction, while in those cases where a tree had fallen since the last vehicle had passed, the driver was left to solve the question in accordance with his own judgment.

Another troublesome condition arose from the frequent intersection of this road by the so-called "log roads,"—roads cut for the purpose of removing the white pine mill-logs which had been recently cut in this section. These roads resembled greatly the one on which we were now travelling, and consequently, in the existing darkness, we found ourselves wandering off into these by-roads. In order to avoid as far as possible this annoyance, the photographer, George Ross, and myself kept in advance, lighting our way as well as we could with matches, moving along cautiously, with one or both hands extended before our eyes when left in total darkness. In spite of these precautions we strayed frequently from the proper road off on these by-roads, often calling to each other in order to prevent too great separation. In the mean while Wellington remained by the wagon to assist our youthful driver.

Nearly two hours had been spent in this toilsome manner when a shout from the photographer announced the glad tidings that he had found a log cabin that was inhabited. He called loudly to me; I shouted back to him, having strayed off on a log road about one-fourth of a mile from the road leading to Pickerel Lake (the road that we wished to follow), but failed to make myself heard by Mr. Mildenberger, although I heard him. He had learned at the cabin that we were just above Sphynx Shoot, or Falls, and that the river was only a few rods from the cabin and to the right of the road.

The photographer was now joyful; he rushed into the woods in search of the author, shouting at the top of his voice, "This way! This way!" I soon succeeded in making him understand, and then shouted back to him, "Stand where you are!" He did not obey the injunction, but continued to advance towards me. We were soon so near each other as to be able to speak in an ordinary voice, while at the same time we could easily understand each other. We finally met, and he conducted me back to the cabin. We found this surrounded by a few acres of newly-cleared land, the clearing extending to the river, and even to the point above the falls that we desired to reach.

The wagon, accompanied by Wellington, came up soon after our return, but George Ross could be heard plunging through the brush a few rods from the road. He, too, had, like myself, strayed off on a wood road, but had heard the photographer's shouts, and these guided his return. The fence surrounding the clearing was opened so as to allow our wagon to enter; we were bound to reach the river to-night. The horse and wagon passed cautiously over the cleared fields, while Wellington held his post on the right of the wagon, and George had taken a position on the left.

Our canoes and other luggage had reached the objective-point and were quickly taken from the wagon. The boy driver had quietly unharnessed his horse and turned him loose to graze in the field. The chief cultivated articles now remaining ungathered in this clearing were the turnips. I asked the boy how he was to get back to Burk's Falls to-night. He replied, "I shan't try to get back there to-night. Ise going to stay with you all." The reply to the brave boy was, "That is right. We will give you something to eat, and you can make a bed on the ground where we all sleep."

A large pile of logs was found which had been heaped up for burning when the ground was cleared; but the fire had failed to consume them, consequently it was only necessary to rearrange them and apply the match. This was done; *a grand illumination followed, the field was lighted around us, the silvery surface of the river was now visible; a good supper was quickly made ready, a rubber poncho was spread on the ground and served as a table; we ate, drank, and were happy.* When the meal was finished we spread our blankets on the ground, and with the starry canopy above us were able to sleep soundly without canvas or any other artificial shelter.

The boy remained with us, enjoying well the food, but when our blankets were spread out he showed, by his manner, a disinclination to camp in the open air, and soon after said, "I think I will go to the cabin; I have a cousin there." He immediately started off, returning a little after daylight the next morning. He breakfasted with us, harnessed his horse, and was off at an early hour for Burk's Falls.

When thinking of the boy's coolness and forethought, I could not avoid comparing him with our city boys of the same age, and the only comment which I will here make is, that this youthful driver is now receiving an education that prepares him thoroughly for a life in this wild country.

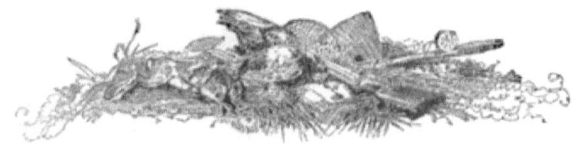

## CHAPTER VII.

THE MOVEMENTS OF OUR HUNTING-PARTY—CROSSING THE HOR-KA-POR-KA PORTAGE—FISHING IN ROCK LAKE—ANOTHER ADVANCE—DEER-HUNTING, ETC.—THE JOURNEY FROM TROUT LAKE TO LONG LAKE—CAMP ON LONG LAKE—MORE DEER-HUNTING—AN EXCITING CONTEST, IN WHICH THE PHOTOGRAPHER WINS.

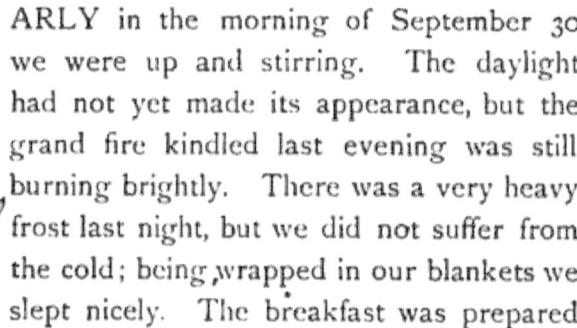

ARLY in the morning of September 30 we were up and stirring. The daylight had not yet made its appearance, but the grand fire kindled last evening was still burning brightly. There was a very heavy frost last night, but we did not suffer from the cold; being wrapped in our blankets we slept nicely. The breakfast was prepared by our guides; the photographer and myself had made our morning toilets while standing on a rock that projected into the river, having brought to this spot soap, towels, tooth-brushes, hair-brushes, combs, etc. This labor was performed in the gray dawn of the morning, and when completed we repaired to the breakfast, which had been spread for us on the rubber poncho in the usual style.

The packing of our luggage followed our morning meal. The canoes were placed in the water and loaded ready for the start. It had been previously decided that the photographer and myself should walk through the woods to Pickerel Lake, while the guides paddled the canoes up the river to the same point. The only difficulty that we anticipated was that of following the stream through the wilderness up to the lake. It is true that we were provided with a compass, but this instrument possessed little value for us here, since there was some question in regard to the direction we ought to take. The lake was thought to be distant from Sphynx Falls about five miles, and it was considered very desirable to reach it at an early hour in the day, in order that we might cross over to Mossup's Landing and make a start the same day on the crossing of the Hor-ka-por-ka Portage. The guides before pushing the canoes from the shore that morning at Sphynx Falls gave us such information as they possessed, and when the good-by had been said they were off on the water, and we turned into the forest. We found some *ruffed grouse*, but no other game during our morning tramp.

We wandered about much in the wilderness, and visited the river frequently to determine whether we were travelling in the right direction. Thus we were enabled to determine our course, and finally reached Harvey's Bridge, near Pickerel Lake, about one o'clock P.M.

Few incidents occurred during this long walk, and none of sufficient importance to be worthy of mention here. The morning was bright and beautiful, but before noon clouds had made their appearance and rain began to fall. The rain, however, did not continue for more than two hours, when the sun reappeared and filled our hearts with joy This walk had been through the woods, including swamps and rocky hills, while our pathway was obstructed with much fallen timber.

We had expected to meet our guides at Harvey's Bridge, where they had agreed to await our arrival, should they reach that point in advance of us; therefore their absence at the time of our arrival satisfied us that we were in the advance. It was nearly an hour before they made their appearance with the luggage and canoes. We immediately took places in the bark canoes, and were paddled over to Mossup's Landing, the southern extremity of the Hor-ka-por-ka Portage, which connects Pickerel Lake with Rock Lake; points which are said to be distant from each other only three miles, but I am sure that I walked more than six miles the first time that I made the tour.

The portage crosses over the top of Ball Mountain, and as you approach Rock Lake you are compelled to traverse an alder swamp about one-half mile in width. This portage has been greatly improved since I crossed for the first time, in 1880. The underbrush has been cut out and some of the more troublesome obstructions overcome, or at least greatly lessened.

The southern end of this portage is now passable for an ox-team with a jumper for a distance somewhat less than a mile; consequently we had hoped to find Mossup able to give us a start on this part of our journey with his oxen. In this matter, however, we were doomed to disappointment, inasmuch as our friend was not provided with the necessary vehicle. The luggage, including the canoes, with which we were now burdened, it was thought would weigh about one thousand pounds,—no unimportant impedimenta; and, consequently, the task of transporting all this across the portage seemed formidable to us when we learned from Mossup that he could not render assistance with his team.

The guides had firmly counted on this aid, and for this purpose sought out Mossup immediately after our arrival at this end of the portage. I did not deem it wise to hesitate, nor to attempt to transfer our luggage to Rock Lake without additional assistance; and therefore immediately employed Mossup and his son to aid us in making the transit. This question having been settled, we started off with our packs, properly arranged, to travel as much of the Hor-ka-por-ka Portage as we might before nightfall. The guides selected a camping-ground about three-fourths of a mile from Mossup's Landing, and made two trips over this portion of the portage. The photographer and myself did not return with them when they made the second trip, but went in search of ruffed grouse, which were found in great abundance around Mossup's small clearing. We spent a pleasant night in camp, and were moving with the first appearance of the gray day in the morning.

Having learned on the previous evening that there was another settler in the vicinity of Mossup's who would probably be willing to assist us in portaging, I sent for him, and he made his appearance in camp very soon after daylight, joined us at our breakfast, and tramped with us on the trail. Our party now consisted of seven members, and it was a pleasing sight, when standing on some high mountain rock, to look down on these sturdy men who were toiling patiently up the mountain-side. The author had started out from camp in the morning burdened with two rifles, three shot-guns, and a fishing-rod, while the photographer, who followed him, was carrying a much heavier load. The guides were each supposed to carry a pack weighing about one hundred pounds, and the settler, whom he had just employed, about the same amount. The settler, Emerson, who made his appearance this morning, is the largest man in the party, and he seems to possess about as much strength as an ordinary pack-mule. These backwoodsmen are generally very strong men and thoroughly accustomed to carrying heavy packs, while at the same time they are satisfied with a moderate compensation, one dollar being the amount always demanded when meals are furnished to the laborer.

The chief guide, however, does not rank as a laborer, and he is commonly paid about two dollars and fifty cents or three dollars per diem, furnishing the canoes and the necessary dogs, but his assistants are paid one dollar a day.

It was now the first day of October; the sky was clear and the sun was shining brightly, while we toiled up the side of Ball Mountain, with happy anticipations of grand sport that would amply compensate us for all this toil. In due time we reached the mountain-top, where a halt was called, that we might view the surrounding country and admire its strange beauty. The photographer here determined to take a view showing our party as we appeared at this moment.

This illustration is intended to show the party as they appeared when carrying their burdens on the Ho-ka-por-ka Portage; and, consequently, young Mossup is seen standing beneath the canoe, which is held in the same position as it is carried, while Emerson is supporting on his shoulders

We are ready for the journey.

a sack of flour which weighed one hundred pounds. It should now be understood that we have left civilization behind us; that our eyes are turned towards the grand wilderness which we are about entering, and that within it we are bound to remain six or eight weeks without seeing a human habitation. The photographer has caught up this view—this grand wilderness—and fixed it on paper, that I may present it to the interested reader who has concluded to follow us in our ramble,—to camp with us in the forest.

The author and the photographer reached Rock Lake about eleven o'clock, closely followed by the guides and their assistants; but this was only their first trip, while one-half of our luggage still remained on the top of the mountain. Consequently, after a brief rest, Wellington, George, Emerson, and Mossup, Sr., returned to bring up the balance. I retained young Mossup to paddle a canoe for me while I fished in the lake.

The trout-fishing was grand, and I caught a fine lot of these beauties, while the photographer was taking a view of this lake and the guides and their assistants were bringing down the balance of our luggage.

We dined about two o'clock, on lake-trout, just taken from the water. After dinner, Emerson, Mossup, and son returned to their homes, while our party proceeded to cross Rock Lake, which is connected by a half-mile portage with Mud Lake. We reached the latter lake about four o'clock, but much of our luggage remained behind on Rock Lake and must be brought over this half-mile portage before we can proceed farther on our journey.

We succeeded in crossing Mud Lake, and camped on

the portage between the latter and Loon Lake. Mud Lake is a small body of water, probably about half a mile in length, and the portage which connects this lake with Loon Lake does not much exceed the same distance.

Captain George Ross, who had parted with us at the village of Maganetawan to hunt up his dogs which had strayed away, joined us this morning, October 2, in our camp near Mud Lake, before we had breakfasted. He has brought the dogs back with him, and we can now engage in a deer-hunt whenever it is thought best. Still-hunting is impracticable until the leaves have fallen, which has not yet occurred, and consequently the dogs are required for the purpose of enabling us to provide for the wants of our camp.

We broke camp at an early hour and started off for Loon Lake, which was reached in due time. This lake is probably a little more than two miles in length, and is separated from Grass Lake by a narrow strip of land which does not exceed more than eight rods in width; consequently the portage is traversed in a few moments.

The captain brought to our camp this morning another canoe. We have with us at this time three canoes. The luggage was promptly carried over to Loon Lake this morning, loaded into our canoes, in which we promptly embarked, and were paddled by our guides up the lake to the narrow neck of land, which has been previously mentioned; crossed the same, and at once started forward on the smooth water of Grass Lake. We encamped at one o'clock on the west shore of this body of water, near its northern extremity. The camp is situated in the woods, only a few rods from the water's edge, thus affording a very picturesque view of the lake and rising sun. It required only a few moments to erect our tent and make the camp, and the next labor which followed was the preparation of the dinner. This was disposed of and a deer-hunt promptly inaugurated by Wellington, who started into the woods with the dogs about three o'clock in the afternoon. The captain and Mildenberger watched the northern extremity of the lake while George and I went to the southern part of the same. These points are separated by something more than one mile; nevertheless we heard distinctly the sound of Mildenberger's gun when *he shot the deer just as it broke from cover* and before it entered the water.

The author soon after this returned to camp, where he found the happiest man on the American continent (at that particular moment), an amateur sportsman, who had just won his grandest triumph,—had killed larger game than can now be found in any part of Germany. The ambitious military officer *who has just won his first grand victory could not be happier.*

The photographer in his childhood dreams had never anticipated so grand a success as a sportsman. The deer that he had just killed was not ruthlessly slaughtered in the water, but was struck by the deadly missile while still in the air, and only a few seconds after it broke cover.

It is now fashionable for our sporting papers to condemn entirely the use of dogs in deer-hunting, not even admitting that the question is one which might properly be discussed; thus certain harpists seek to become authorities in all these matters.

"He shot the deer just as it broke from cover."

Every sportsman will cheerfully admit that the taking of game ought to be restricted within certain limits. What are these limits? In order to speak intelligently on this question it is very necessary that the speaker should be familiar with the localities in which the game is found, the various methods employed for its capture, the necessities of the people inhabiting the game regions, and the condition of the game at the various seasons at which it is hunted. In those localities where the game is already very scarce it may be highly important for the sportsman and other interested parties to limit, *or even entirely stop, the destruction for certain periods.*

Although the interests of the sportsman are commonly identical with those of the inhabitants residing in game countries, nevertheless the necessities of the latter may be such as to know no bounds. In the district of Muskoka, Canada, it is safe to assert that fifty deer are killed by the still-hunters where one is killed after having been run by dogs, either on the run-ways or in the water. The deer killed on the run-ways and in the water are usually consumed in the sportsman's camp, and if the price of this venison were determined by the money outlay made by this class of men while seeking the game, it would probably vary from twenty-five cents to one dollar per pound.

The deer killed by the still-hunter in this region is generally consumed in the lumber camps, where it is sold for four or five cents per pound.

The great body of the sportsmen entering the district of Muskoka are residents of the United States, and would not remain in this climate during the cold months of autumn and winter, when still-hunting can be advantageously practised; while the venison is in better condition during September than in any other month of the year. Furthermore, the music of the hounds when running deer gives an additional pleasure to the sportsman. In this section of country, were it possible to prevent the sale of venison in lumber camps, the deer, which are now very abundant, would soon become more numerous than sheep have ever been on the hills of Vermont, even though the pioneer hunters are permitted to kill deer at will, and the true sportsman allowed to continue to hound the game.

It has not been my intention to discuss thoroughly the question that I raised; this would require more time and space than I can give to the consideration of the subject; but I desired rather to direct the reader's attention to it, hoping thereby to arouse thought on this and other kindred topics.

We continued the deer-hunt on October 3, notwithstanding a drizzling rain, which continued to fall during the most of the day. This day there were two deer killed, although I find that nothing happened of any particular interest or worthy of notice here. The following day Wellington Ross, who had been with us almost constantly since our arrival in the district of Muskoka, took his departure for home. He had shared with us the pleasures of the hunt and served us faithfully as a guide. The other members of the party engaged during the forenoon in an unsuccessful deer-hunt. The afternoon was spent by the photographer and George in making negatives about the lake, while the captain went with me in search of ruffed grouse, in which we were, however, unsuccessful, ruffed grouse not being as abundant here as they were about Mossup's and Rock Lake. During our stay on these lakes we discovered a beaver-house which was at this time occupied by a family of beavers. I spent a part of one evening with the captain watching for this interesting family, the members of which never, or at least very rarely, make their appearance in the waters about their house much before sunset. We arrived on the water in proximity to this dwelling at the proper time, but failed to see the beaver, although the captain says the acute animal saw us. The statement was based on the fact that we heard a sound which the captain recognized as the beaver's alarm-signal, which is followed by the rapid disappearance of the master of ceremonies, who neither reappears nor permits any of the members to show themselves for several hours after the alarm has been sounded. We remained here, keeping perfectly quiet for about an hour, but heard nothing more.

It was after dark when we reached the camp, but we were informed on our return that a flock of wild geese had passed over it, going southward. The sight of the geese so affected George Ross that he caught up his Winchester rifle and sent several bullets after them, although the photographer thinks that their flying was not in any manner inconvenienced by the shooting of our guide.

The afternoon of the 5th of October was spent in making preparations for our departure on the morning of the 6th for Long Lake. We had killed more deer while in this camp than we had consumed. The captain placed one-half of the largest deer that we had killed in his canoe and carried it to a poor widow who lived several miles from the camp. He also sent for other settlers, who appeared and carried away all our surplus game. Consequently, on the morning of the 6th, we were ready to strike our tents and move forward to new fields of sport.

There had been a thunder-storm during the night prior to our departure, but the morning was clear, with a strong breeze. We broke camp about 8.20 A.M. and went to the head of Grass Lake, *en route* for Long Lake, reaching the latter point at one o'clock, having crossed three small lakes and four short portages. We dined at the foot of this lake, and after dinner paddled up to the head of the same, where we encamped. Our camp is very pleasantly situated in a dense forest, but also quite near the lake-shore. During the afternoon the captain and myself took a stroll about a beaver-dam at the head of the lake in search of beaver. We succeeded in finding one family here. We also trolled a portion of the time that we were absent from camp, and caught six fine lake-trout.

We are now in the virgin forest, where the lumberman has not destroyed its original beauty by the removal of a single pine-tree. Here we see nature in all her wildness and enchanting beauty. Here the landscape is clothed in nature's robes of green during the spring and summer months, dotted here and there with her silvery lakes and rivers, while in autumn she adds to these charming colors her lovely golden tints.

The lover of nature cannot resist the grandeur, the enchanting beauty, and overwhelming sense of his obligations to Deity, when he travels along nature's highways and views this magnificent scenery. It is a more eloquent and forcible sermon than has ever been preached from any pulpit in Christendom.

It is, to me, a sincere regret that I cannot picture to the mind of the reader the beauty and grandeur of these scenes; and likewise that I cannot convey to him the unspeakable pleasures and the gratitude which I felt while worshipping at nature's shrine in these grand forests. I sincerely wish that the whole world could enjoy these things as I enjoyed them; but neither the author nor the photographer can present them with nature's power.

Having spent the day very pleasantly, surrounded with novel scenes, we retired early to our tents for repose; but sounds which were novel to my ears soon aroused me from my slumbers, and I listened more than half an hour to the mingled howlings of a pack of wolves. These animals are not dangerous to mankind; they differ widely from European wolves, and are principally troublesome in this country because of their sheep-killing proclivities. This music that we heard to-night, the howling of the wolves, was repeated every night for more than a month; in fact, we heard it nightly as long as we remained in this dark wilderness.

These serenades were the only evidences we had of their existence, until after the snow had fallen so as to render perceptible their tracks, which were then occasionally discovered.

The forenoon of the next day, October 7, was spent in trout-fishing, grouse-shooting, and exploring the surrounding country. The captain conducted me about half a mile up the side of a steep hill, which had its base on Long Lake, to another lake situated on the top of this hill or mountain. While I recognize the fact that all mountain lakes occupy different planes or levels, some higher and others lower, still it seemed very unusual to climb the face of a steep hill, commencing at one lake, and find another just where you had expected to reach the hill-top. This lake was nearly round and probably somewhat less than one-half mile in diameter. We saw, during our morning peregrinations, many old moose-tracks, and also many spots in the woods where these animals had browsed; while a few of these moose indications were certainly of recent origin.

The captain thought it wise to tarry in our present camp several days, to kill deer and dry the venison, in order that we might have a supply of meat while engaged in moose-hunting, independent of that which we might be able to kill during this period.

We had unanimously agreed that it was inexpedient to take dogs with us on the moose chase. In this particular our experience fully confirmed the wisdom of our conclusion. The moose cannot be driven to water by deer-hounds, or any other species of dogs with which I am familiar; and, therefore, had we taken these animals with us, they could only have served to announce our presence to the game which we sought, without being able to render any assistance. These facts will become more apparent to the reader when he has read other portions of this book, when the story of the moose-hunt has been told from beginning to end. We are now entering on nature's grandest preserve,—we find here the "King of the Canadian Forest," alias moose, deer, beaver, black bear, black wolf, speckled- and lake-trout, duck, ruffed grouse, etc. Here is abundance of sport for the true sportsman. During the morning stroll we saw several beaver-houses which were occupied, and examined a large amount of their fresh work. These sights were highly interesting to me, but inasmuch as they have been so frequently described by others, I shall omit them here.

It was already after twelve o'clock when we reached our camp. The guides prepared our dinner, which was speedily partaken of, and then we got off on a deer-hunt. The captain started into the woods with the dogs. George Ross and I entered a canoe, the former paddling across the lake to a point that commanded a view of a large portion of this water. We then stepped on dry land, and there patiently awaited the coming developments. We carefully scanned every visible portion of the lake. An hour passed and still we were watching; soon a grand splash was heard near the shore on the opposite side of the lake; the guide caught sight of the water which was thrown high into the air, but the head of the deer was scarcely visible to him while the animal was swimming towards us. The deer, which, at first, swam directly towards us, soon changed his course and headed towards the foot of the lake. This change brought him plainly into view. A few minutes later the dog was seen running from the woods where the deer broke cover. The head and antlers of our game were visible above the waters of the lake, while he was swimming majestically without fear or even anxiety. We stood nearly half an hour watching the movements of this deer, since we could not safely move lest we should be discovered by the game and give him an opportunity to return to his forest home. The reader should remember that this animal took to the water from the shore nearly opposite to the point on which we were standing, that the deer swam almost directly towards us until he reached the middle of the stream, then turned downward, which gave us, in due time, an opportunity to come in unperceived behind him. Patiently we awaited this opportune moment. When it arrived, the canoe, which had been drawn up on the shore near us, was quietly shoved out upon the water. Ross gently stepped to the stern with his paddle in hand, steadied our little bark while I entered its bow, where I seated myself and placed my rifle at my right side. Ross carefully pushed the little craft from its moorings, placed himself on his knees in that part of the canoe which properly trimmed it, and silently plied his paddle.

The little canoe moved noiselessly but rapidly forward, every stroke of the paddle bringing us nearer to the game. There was another paddle lying near my hand; I seized it and gave a helping hand, greatly increasing the speed. Forward, forward we went! We were unperceived, although within ten rods of a beautiful buck, which was swimming in the middle of the lake directly before us. My paddle was changed for my rifle. Nearer, still nearer we approached. The rifle was raised; the bead was drawn, just below the base of the animal's skull. We were six rods distant from the deer. A little puff of white smoke covered the bow of our boat; the crack of the rifle was heard, and the lifeless body of the deer floated on the water, which was slightly tinged with blood. Thus ended this chase. The carcass was towed to shore in front of our camp, and the captain met us there, having returned from the woods, where he had gone to start the dogs. The dog which followed the buck that I had just shot was also now in our camp, but the other was still absent. Nearly two hours had elapsed since the buck was shot. There were now on the shore, in front of our camp, the captain, George Ross, and myself, while Mildenberger had gone back into the forest in search of ruffed grouse. Suddenly the captain sprang from the rock on which he had been seated, placed his right hand on his forehead in such a position as to shade his eyes, while he leaned slightly forward and gazed steadily out over the surface of the lake a few seconds without uttering a single word. This position was one that I had frequently seen him assume. I therefore recognized the fact that he had sighted game, or was at least swayed by this thought, and now endeavored to solve the question. Thus he had stood for a few seconds, when he simply exclaimed, "*A deer in the lake!*" and instantly sprang forward to the canoe. I had followed him closely with rifle in hand, expecting to make the chase with him; he quickly pushed the frail bark into the water and hastily said, "Doctor, let George go with me in the canoe; it will be a hard chase; we will drive the deer to you." A few seconds later the canoe was on the water, the captain in the bow and George Ross in the stern, each on their knees with a paddle in their hands. The little birch-bark was rushing rapidly forward, propelled by the power of four strong, muscular arms. The sight is a grand one, and called to mind the impetuous charge of a squadron of cavalry in war times. The captain is most determined and energetic when in the pursuit of game; like the grandest charger in the squadron, he is bound to take the lead, while the others can only follow.

This peculiarity of the man has been demonstrated frequently in my presence in the chase, and all his fellow-huntsmen and guides are ready to grant him this position. I had seated myself on a rock, soon after the departure of the guides, to watch the deer, whose head was visible to me in my position, although fully a mile away. I could not, however, at so great a distance, determine whether this animal possessed antlers or not; but the leisurely manner in which it was swimming satisfied me its pursuers were undiscovered until they had made at least three-fourths of the whole distance. The animal, when first discovered, was nearly opposite to our camp and within a few rods of the farther shore. The guides, in order to succeed in the accomplishment of their purpose, were compelled to make a considerable detour to the rear of the animal, and finally come up between it and the shore. Fortunately for us they had remained, for a considerable time, undiscovered, and the animal, in the mean time, was gradually leaving the shore while swimming down the lake. The moment, however, came when the pursuers were discovered, and *the deer then made the most frantic efforts. I could see it spring forward with all its power, raising its* head high in the air with each grand effort, but the guides are pulling stronger than before on their paddles. They seem, when viewed from my position, to be only a few rods in the rear of the animal, but the deer is heading for the shore and seems about ready to bound into the forest. It is now evident to me that the chase can only last a few seconds. *I sprang from my seat; I recalled the fact that the guides have no gun in the boat; I realize that if they had one they could now easily kill the animal; they are almost on it. An instant later and the canoe is seen between the deer and the shore; a loud shout is heard from the guides; they wave their hats; they are victorious, and the disappointed deer now turns and swims towards the middle of the lake. Its grandest effort has been made; fatigue and disappointment slow down its movements.* It was now an easy task for the guides to direct the animal to any point on the lake. The canoe was kept in the rear, and when it was brought forward towards the right of the deer, it would cause the animal to oblique to the left, and *vice versa*. In this manner they proceeded to cross the lake, bringing the doe in front of the rock on which I was seated; but while she was still about six hundred yards away they called on me to take a shot. I demurred against their request, inasmuch as the portion of the animal now visible did not much exceed the dimensions of a pint cup. The first ball fired fell short about fifty yards, and then ricochetted nearly across the lake. Another shot was fired with no better result, and thus I continued for several minutes, but not without making some improvement. The shots were pronounced by the guides to be accurate, so far as the line of the target was concerned, but the balls still fell short of the mark.

The photographer, who was absent in the woods when I commenced firing, now made his appearance, and seizing the Winchester rifle, began to compete with me. He was able to fire two shots with the repeater while I could fire one from the breech-loading Ballard. The contest between us was now very lively, and we succeeded in persuading the guides to bring the game nearer to us, so that the animal was not more than one hundred yards from the muzzles of the rifles. The bullets now fell in very close proximity to the doe's head; none were more than four or five inches from its centre. Six or eight shots have been fired with this degree of accuracy, when I send in one that breaks the skin over the base of the animal's skull. She dodges her head downward, but quickly brings it up again, when a shot from Mildenberger ends this trial of skill. *The guides shout aloud and lustily cheer the photographer, who proudly puts down his rifle and wipes the perspiration from his brow.*

## CHAPTER VIII.

DRYING VENISON—A GRAND AND BEAUTIFUL MOUNTAIN GORGE—THE MEETING AT THE BEAVER-DAM—OUR PHOTOGRAPHER LOST IN THE WILDERNESS—A LONELY NIGHT ON BUCK LAKE—THE HORRIBLE DREAM—THE LOST MAN FOUND—THE UNEXPECTED MEETING WITH A BULL MOOSE.

THE preparation for the moose-hunt was now commenced by cutting the flesh of the deer, which we had just killed, into strips or slices, and drying the same on a scaffold erected for the purpose over our camp-fire. This labor, however, did not interfere seriously with the continuation of deer-hunting, trout-fishing, and bird-shooting; but, inasmuch as we have fully described these sports, we shall hereafter entirely omit, or pass very rapidly over, them, lest a too frequent repetition of that which is very interesting may become monotonous.

We remained on this lake ten days, during which period the venison was fully dried, and we had a very enjoyable time. The weather was generally very pleasant, although we had a slight snow-storm and occasional rains. The photographer took many negatives, and among others, a view of our camp, which appears as a frontispiece in this book. Game was found here in great abundance, and our larder was always well supplied; in fact, there was no time during our stay on this lake when we had not plenty of venison, trout, and ruffed grouse; nor was it found necessary for us to spend more than a small portion of our time in procuring these necessities; consequently, both long and short journeys were made into the surrounding forest with no other object than spending our time pleasantly. It should, nevertheless, be here confessed that nature frequently rewarded us for these labors, even beyond our expectations, revealing to us at such times her grandest secrets. It was during our stay on this lake that the photographer and I started out one afternoon, taking with us bird-dogs and shot-guns, although the chief object of this trip was not to gather in partridges for food, but rather to study nature in this grand solitude. We walked together probably about one mile, chatting pleasantly in the mean time, when I separated from him for the purpose of investigating a deep and dark ravine, which I was at that moment entering. The desire to be alone, entirely alone, so far as human companionship was concerned, had taken complete possession of my soul. I therefore informed Mr. Mildenberger that we would separate here, and that I would rejoin him at the head of the lake. Two bird-dogs remained with me, while one accompanied the photographer; *even this companionship was now more than I desired.* Faithful Ponto commonly afforded me much satisfaction by his persevering efforts to find game, and little Romp often amused me by his wild antics; but that afternoon I frequently wished that they were both back in camp.

The sun was shining brightly, but nevertheless the depth of the ravine which I had entered was so great, and the shadows of the giant trees which overhung its borders so dark, that I soon found myself in a sort of twilight. This peculiar light gave a strange and weird appearance to those objects situated at the bottom of the ravine, while the autumnal frosts had touched the foliage of the trees growing from its sides, as well as those which overhung it, imparting to it many of the most beautiful colors of the rainbow, which it rivalled in beauty. Great rocks and grand boulders, frequently covered with ferns, were often seen in the bottom and on the sides of this half-lighted chasm. *Grandeur and beauty were here combined.* As I proceeded up this mountain gorge, the scenes presented were truly kaleidoscopic: the surrounding landscape presented an endless variety of beautiful colors, which a marvellous play of light and shade blended in the formation of pictures that were frequently artistic, although at other times they were grotesque and comical.

Slowly I advanced through this fairy-land, often halting, and sometimes seating myself on some convenient rock in order to study more carefully the effect of a passing cloud, or the flight of a bird which chanced to come in such a position as to throw its shadow within my view. In this manner the time passed rapidly, and my promise to meet the photographer at the head of the lake had been completely forgotten. It was not until late in the afternoon that I was stimulated, by the increasing darkness in the deep, dark mountain gorge, to quicken my pace, in order that I might be able to return to camp before nightfall.

Finally, hurried forward by the thought that I might be compelled to spend a night in the woods, where the charming scenes just described had been dispelled by the increasing gloom, I soon found myself at the end of the gorge and on the top of the mountain. The entire length of this deep ravine did not exceed two miles, but I had spent within it more than three hours. Having reached the mountain-top, I was now convinced that I had an abundance of time to return to our camp by the way of the head of the lake; and I was prompted to start in this direction by the belief that Mr. Mildenberger would probably remain in that vicinity until I could join him. It now remained for me to determine the direction which I must take in order to reach this objective-point. I seated myself for a few moments, thought on the subject, and then proceeded on my journey, but had not taken a dozen steps when I caught an instantaneous glance of a fine buck not more than forty yards from me on the slope of the mountain. This animal rushed down the mountain-side with such rapidity that I was unable to get a distinct outline of his form at any time after he had taken his first leap, although the movements of the underbrush and a shadowy figure were visible for a few seconds. Romp started promptly after the fleeing animal, and Ponto soon joined in the chase. The direction taken by these fugitives was towards the head of the lake, and therefore I followed after them. I had tramped, I supposed, about two miles, when I came to a cedar swamp, which I unhesitatingly penetrated, and soon found myself standing on the edge of a considerable brook, which I thought would enter the lake near the head of that body of water; consequently, I started down this stream, which I followed about two miles, when I heard a shout from the photographer. I was delighted to hear his voice, but greatly surprised to find him in such a dense jungle. I had previously observed that the brook which I was following had overflowed its borders,—had, evidently, quite recently assumed unusual proportions, since the trees now nearly submerged were still apparently healthy.

It is a well-known fact to backwoodsmen that trees when com-

Beaver-dam and house.

pletely submerged soon die. I was not, therefore, surprised when the photographer, whom I had approached so nearly as to now be within speaking distance, although

I could not yet see the objects which were immediately about him, said, "I am standing on a recently-constructed beaver-dam, while the beaver-house, not yet fully completed, is situated very near."

I finally succeeded in reaching the spot where my photographer was standing, learned that he had been there two or three hours, that the bird-dogs had been in his company a considerable portion of this time, having evidently followed the deer which I had seen on the top of the mountain into this vicinity. Mr. Mildenberger was evidently greatly interested in the labors of this animal, and while contemplating it had forgotten the lake. He failed to give me any information in regard to the route by which he had reached his present situation. It was, therefore, necessary to follow the brook down to the lake, which feat was successfully accomplished; in fact, the task was not very difficult when we had succeeded in getting below the dam, where the stream once more possessed its natural boundaries, although its course led us through a very dense growth of alders and other swamp vegetation.

The lake was reached soon after sunset, and the firing of a few signal-guns brought the guides with the canoes promptly to us on the shore, where we had already built a fire for the purpose of revealing our whereabouts.

There occurred on Tuesday, October 10, while we were encamped on Long Lake, one of the most exciting events of our sojourn in the forest, although it was only fortunate in its happy termination. Captain Ross and the photographer started this morning into the woods, the former for the purpose of starting a deer, while the latter was intent on shooting ruffed grouse. We were somewhat surprised when the captain reached us, about one o'clock in the afternoon, unaccompanied by Mr. Mildenberger, inasmuch as the latter possessed no knowledge of woodcraft, and was therefore extremely liable to become confused and fail to reach our camp. It had also been observed that the photographer was entirely indifferent in regard to danger in this particular; and even Wellington Ross, prior to separating from us, had expressed the opinion that Mr. Mildenberger would yet be compelled to spend one or more nights in the wilderness without the society of his comrades.

The moment the captain reached camp this afternoon he inquired if the photographer had returned, and when answered in the negative, he expressed considerable anxiety. He said, "I left him early in the morning, and expected to find him near the spot where we had separated when I returned there about one hour since; but he had taken his departure and could not be found. I then thought that probably he had grown weary of waiting for me and had retraced his steps to the lake, fired a signal for a canoe, and thus reached the camp."

Immediately after dinner the guides started out in search of the lost photographer, each having arranged with the other to go in a different direction, in order to cover as much space as possible before nightfall, while they carried with them their guns, which they continued to fire at intervals for the purpose of attracting Mr. Mildenberger's attention and aiding him in finding the camp. The search was earnestly kept up during the whole afternoon, and only terminated with the commencing darkness of evening, while the firing of guns was continued until nine o'clock. This firing since nightfall was stimulated by certain indistinct sounds heard by us, which we thought to be the shouts of the lost photographer, although there was some doubt in our minds on this subject.

The anxiety felt in our camp for our lost companion is very great this evening. It is greatly feared that he will attempt to travel in the woods at night. This effort might be productive of fatal results. Again, it is thought possible that fear and anxiety may possibly affect his intellect, and thus cause him to wander away from the sounds of our guns and otherwise interfere with us in our search and his safe return to camp. The reader, in order to fully comprehend the fears and anxieties of those in camp, must remember that the lost man was a complete stranger to our country, a German, whose knowledge of a wilderness had been gained from a few acres of woodland in his boyhood home, or possibly a small park containing trees and small streams. Furthermore, his residence in America since his arrival on these shores has been limited entirely to large cities, with no knowledge of our rural districts at the time he started on this journey. The anxiety which we felt for his safety was likewise intimately connected with the objects which we desired to accomplish by this journey into the wilderness. The author had started from his home with the determination of engaging in a grand moose-hunt before he returned, and had employed the photographer that he might be able to present to his friends in the future some pleasant reminiscences of the doings of his party in the Lake Lands of Canada. The party was now just about engaging in the chief object of the expedition. It will, therefore, be observed that both sympathy and self-interest combined to increase our solicitude for the safety of Mr. Mildenberger.

The fruitless search for the missing man during the afternoon had served to greatly increase this anxiety; and therefore the entire conversation around our camp-fire during the evening related to a further prosecution of the search for the photographer. This subject was thoroughly discussed, and it was finally agreed that the captain should start from camp in the morning with the earliest dawn of day, and that George Ross and the author should follow as soon as it became evident to them that the captain's first effort had failed. The captain, during the discussion which occurred in the evening around the camp-fire, had expressed the opinion that Mr. Mildenberger would be found in the morning at Mountain Lake. In our contemplation of the condition of the photographer, we were comforted by the thought that the weather was now clear and mild, and therefore he would be relieved from the physical sufferings that might otherwise attend a separation from us. We were likewise aware that he was supplied with matches, which would enable him to build a fire, and thus render his surroundings in the woods more endurable at night than they would otherwise have been.

The author spent a restless night in his tent; his sleep was disturbed; his companion was absent, and there was some doubt as to his safety. He awoke before it was light; awaited rather anxiously the first dawn of day, which made its appearance about 5.45, when he called the captain and asked him if it was not time to start on the search. The captain rubbed his eyes and replied in the affirmative. We then both arose and stepped from our respective tents into the open air. At that moment we heard the voice of Mr. Mildenberger. It was indistinct; he evidently was a great distance from us, but we both now felt assured that he was still alive. We recognized the voice as that of our photographer. The captain quickly fired two shots, hoping that Mr. Mildenberger would hear the sound; and then he promptly started for the shore where his canoe was lying; the little bark was shoved off on the water, and, occupied by our sturdy backwoodsman, she glided away on the smooth surface of the lake with great rapidity. We listened intently to the shots fired from the captain's rifle, and also to his lusty shouts. We had expected that these sounds would elicit a reply from our lost friend, but no answer was heard. The captain paddled quickly across the lake; the canoe was drawn on the shore; the sound of his voice and the report of his rifle were heard more than half an hour after he entered the woods; but both gradually grew less distinct, and finally were heard no more. We had expected to hear some answering shots or shouts from Mr. Mildenberger, but none have reached our ears since the early dawn. Is he wandering away from us? Has he failed to hear our shots? These were the questions asked in our camp. George has prepared our breakfast and we have attempted to supply nature's demand. We found little pleasure around our board this morning; could not enjoy our food; two of our members are absent, the captain and Mr. Mildenberger, and when will they be with us again? The latter query, like those so recently asked, could not now be answered. It has been more than three hours since the captain left the camp. George was busied with the labors attending the drying of the venison. The author was perched on a high rock at the lake-shore, ready to announce the first appearance of the lost.

The captain's canoe was seen on the lake approaching camp; but the distance was too great for its occupants to be discerned. This discovery was made by the author and promptly announced to the guide in the camp, who immediately came to the lookout.

We are still unable to make out the number of persons in the canoe. Great was our suspense! Great our anxiety to know the result of the captain's search! After a time we were able to distinguish two voices. Gladness filled our hearts; a joyful shout from us was answered by a similar one from the canoe. Two forms are now visible; two paddles are driving the little bark rapidly forward; it will soon be halted at our feet. Shout after shout was heard from our friends, and shout answered shout. Our joy was great and unrestrained. The canoe touched shore, was drawn on dry land, and a joyous handshaking followed. A breakfast was quickly prepared for the photographer and captain. They were hungry, and unquestionably greatly enjoyed the repast.

Let us now return to the photographer's wanderings, and detail his joys and sufferings as he has reported them to us. The morning of the day on which he was lost, when he started out with the captain, was perfectly clear and the sun was shining brightly. He soon found himself thoroughly engrossed in partridge-shooting, and had no thought of danger, or that he should wander away from camp so far that he could not readily find his way back again. He told the captain, when they separated, that he would soon return to the lake; but, since the shooting was very good in the early part of the day, he thought very little of the promise. In fact, he did not think it necessary for him to pay any attention even to the direction in which he was journeying, and consequently he pushed heedlessly forward, passing lake after lake, over mountain and hill, until nearly three o'clock in the afternoon. At this hour he began to feel hungry; halted; dressed and broiled one of the partridges which he had killed in the morning. While thus engaged, it occurred to him that he was lost, and would probably fail to reach camp that night. These thoughts impaired his appetite and rendered him somewhat nervous. The deer-dogs, which the captain had taken with him into the woods in the morning, approached the photographer soon after this lunch. He could not persuade them to remain with him; and, inasmuch as he supposed that they were now returning to camp after their unsuccessful chase, he attempted to follow them; but they were soon lost to his vision. The dogs reached camp before dark, thus succeeding better than Mr. Mildenberger.

The old bird-dog, "Bummer," started with him in the morning, but he too returned to camp. It will, therefore, be observed that the photographer was entirely alone in the wilderness,—that even the dogs had most ungenerously refused to stay with him. When he fully realized that he was lost he walked rapidly, hoping still that he might reach some familiar point in the woods; but everything was strange,—forest, lakes, mountains, and hills all refused to grant the assistance he desired. The anxiety of mind which he felt when he first discovered that he was lost had steadily increased, every hour adding to his sufferings, until he finally found himself plunged into the most intense mental agony. He now realized that he was a stranger in a strange land,—a wanderer in a wilderness so large that it was possible for him to spend several months in wandering without ever coming in contact with a single human being. About an hour before sunset he reached a large lake, or at least one much larger than any he had seen during the day, after leaving the one on which we were encamped. This lake, he thinks, was about two miles in length and about one mile in width. He shot a duck, and then concluded to camp for the night on the shore of this lake. He saw a high cliff at a point on the shore, having a perpendicular rock wall rising more than one hundred and fifty feet above the surface of the lake, and he determined to climb up to this high point and take one more view of terra firma; then, if nothing better offered, he would spend the night there. The cliff, or promontory, which we have mentioned, possessed but one rocky, perpendicular wall; the other sides were steep slopes covered with heavy forest-trees, while there occasionally cropped out a rocky stratum or ledge. These slopes were chiefly covered with a heavy growth of birch and maple, although there were to be seen, near the summit, several large white-pine trees. The photographer had reached the lake-shore about one hundred rods from the southern base of this high cliff, and consequently it required only a few minutes' walk, when he was prepared to commence the ascent. He had walked very rapidly during the latter part of the day, was now greatly fatigued, and consequently he found the ascent of the steep slope very difficult and even painful to him. The steepness of the acclivity was so great that it was impossible for him to make a direct ascent of its face; so he was compelled to tack from one point to another, in imitation of the course pursued by the mariner under certain circumstances. The reader will readily understand that, under these circumstances, it was impossible for the photographer to make very rapid progress in the ascent; still he labored on, drawing himself up by seizing hold of bushes or any other projecting substance, frequently resting in order to gain strength to enable him to make a new effort, and thus, after having spent an hour in this severe toil, he finally reached the summit of the cliff.

Let us now look upon him as he then appeared, after he had accomplished the ascent and stood on the top of the cliff, overlooking the lake and surrounding forest. The reader would have pronounced him, even at this moment, a strong, athletic man, but would have been surprised when he observed that his face was livid, eyes protruding and reddened, forehead, face, and hands covered with large drops of perspiration, while every muscle in the poor sufferer's body trembled from over-exertion. Thus appeared our photographer when he first stepped forward on the high cliff and gazed around him, but only for a few moments, when he was observed to totter and then sink down upon the ground, where he remained prostrate for some minutes, but finally raised himself to a sitting posture. Behold him as he now sat there! partly doubled up, lower extremities extended and resting on the earth, elbows resting on thighs, head drooping forward and clasped on either side with a hand,—a perfect picture of despair. The face is turned towards the earth, the mind is dazed, and he cannot now recall his own doings during the day. Fortunately, this mental condition was of short duration,—lasted only about a quarter of an hour,—when he fully regained consciousness and realized the fact that he was lost. He once more assumed the standing position, and now carefully surveyed the lake and the surrounding landscape. There was nothing visible but this single lake, surrounded by miles and miles of dark forest. He recalled the fact that during this day's journeying he had passed eight or ten lakes, but he observed nothing in the appearance of this wilderness to indicate, at this time, their existence or locality.

The sun had just disappeared behind the western horizon. He now examined the contents of his pockets, and discovered that he had only two cartridges for the shot-gun left. He instantly resolved that he would do no more shooting for the present, unless it became necessary for the preservation of his life. There was no more time to be lost by inactivity, wood must be gathered for the night's fire, and some evergreen boughs placed on the surface of the flat rock in order to prepare it for a seat during his involuntary sojourn. The photographer now set about the performance of these duties, which engaged his attention until the darkness of night had settled down about him.

In the mean while, he had built a fire on the front part

of the plateau, about one hundred feet back from the perpendicular wall which has already been described. This plateau was an oblong piece of ground, containing about one acre, which formed the top of the high cliff, and was covered from near the perpendicular wall which fronted on the lake with whortleberry-bushes and a few dwarfed evergreens, while on the rear of the plateau there were found those trees common to this wilderness.

Having carefully located our photographer where he has concluded to remain until the dawn of the morrow, we are now interested in knowing how he spent the intervening hours. The task has been made easy for the author, he having received a full statement from the photographer, who always seemed anxious to impart to others a knowledge of his feelings and doings on this gloomy night, thus showing a willingness to place his friends in possession of a very valuable experience without their being subjected to the ills from which he suffered. He informed me that, having built the fire, gathered the wood, etc., he then walked to and fro and attempted to collect his thoughts, but could do so only very imperfectly; remembered that he had game in his pockets, but fully realized the fact that he could not eat; was greatly fatigued, but could not sleep. Burdened with his troubles, disappointed and sad, he exclaimed, "What shall I do?" The answer came to him in the twinkling of an eye. "Yell!" and yell he did! It was these tremendous shouts that echoed through the forest, and were heard in our camp between eight and nine o'clock on the evening of the day when our photographer strayed away. These shouts were but indistinctly heard by us; we supposed that they were made by a human being, but there were doubts in our minds on this point. They came to us at intervals of five or ten minutes. We fired guns in response to them, but it made no difference; it did not change even the length of the intervals. We thought it was strange that he did not "yell" immediately after the discharge of our guns. It was strange, but he has since explained all this by saying, "I did not hear your guns; I did not hear your shouts;" and consequently it still seems strange to me that we were able to hear his "yells." These facts can only be explained by some one who possesses a more thorough knowledge of acoustics and our acoustic relations at that moment than your humble servant.

The reader will be still further astonished when he learns that it has been definitely determined since that eventful day that Mr. Mildenberger was separated from us by no less than four English geographical miles. The photographer, having yelled till he was tired of this exercise, still continued to walk, walk, walk! Although sorely fatigued, he was so much disturbed in mind that when he seated himself for a moment he could only remain in that posture for a few seconds. The hours dragged slowly on, midnight came, and he now seated himself before the blazing fire, closed his eyes and did sleep. It was the sleep of exhaustion,—a troubled slumber. In this condition he dreamed that he was a soldier once more; that the fates of war had gone against him. The army to which he belonged had been operating in a wild country; had suffered a most disastrous defeat; the soldiers had fled from the field; had entered a great wilderness, in order to effect escape, but that they were closely pursued by a savage and relentless foe. Listen! He even now hears the shouts of the victors; they have probably picked up some stragglers from the defeated army. A few moments later and he hears a lively discharge of firearms. These sounds are followed by some desultory musket-shots, then all is quiet once more. The photographer now fancies that the victors have come upon a considerable body of his comrades, who have attempted to defend themselves rather than surrender as prisoners of war. He now realizes the imminent danger with which he is surrounded. He imagines that he is fleeing rapidly before the enemy; and we know that he is restless and constantly moving. *Behold him now! His eyes are widely open; he glares wildly about him; still he slumbers. In this disturbed sleep he sees the merciless savage peering from behind every forest-tree and bush upon him.* He calls aloud, "*What shall I do? I am already surrounded.*" He now beholds the *brutal, bloody, and fiendish Iroquois Indians creeping stealthily upon him; they are in full war-paint and armed with their barbarous instruments of war. This is their moment of triumph over a poor defeated Huron! They have risen to their feet, and now rush forward upon our sleeping soldier! The instruments of death are already uplifted; an unearthly yell is heard which echoes from lake to lake!* Our photographer springs to his feet; looks wildly about him. He is now awake; nevertheless he hears a doleful sound: the wolves are howling to-night like so many demons. He had frequently heard them howl, but *never before did their voices sound so near and hateful.* They are no longer musical to his ear, but truly demoniacal to-night. He had been seated by the fire about two hours, but in his horrible dream he had suffered the pangs of a thousand deaths. There was no more slumber for him that night. He would not even seat himself before the fire, but walked again "to and fro," endeavoring to recall the meanderings of the previous day, and to determine upon some plan by which he could return to the camp. The dawn of day finally appeared. His plan was now matured. He would endeavor to retrace his steps; if he could do this, then he could finally reach us once more. The idea that it would become necessary for him to retrace his steps had not occurred to him during his wanderings of the previous day. He had moved off boldly then, trusting to good luck rather than any knowledge of woodcraft to bring him back to us. This man, in fact, had been absolutely reckless in his wanderings since he entered the forest. He did not, apparently, realize that there was danger in straying about the wilderness without the aid of a guide who was familiar with every lake, mountain, and hill.

He had never yet attempted the practice of that precaution which even the best guides frequently take in this grand forest, and which they learned from the Indians. I have frequently observed that my guide, the moment he started from camp, commenced to break the twigs or small branches of the bushes with which he came in contact, carefully turning the broken twig backwards towards the camp, and continued this practice until he was nearly ready to start homeward, when he would face about and return on this trail. This procedure is not practised after the snow has fallen, so long as it remains capable of receiving the impression which makes the trail. Thus we find him suffering from his own neglect; but we feel assured that he is fast learning to live, and we trust that he may live long to learn. Let us now return to him. He is surrounded by the gray dawn of morning; is now ready to attempt to retrace his steps. He utters *one tremendous yell*, which is heard distinctly in our camp, four miles away. He now starts on his return; the captain at the same time sets out in search of him. They met in the woods; it was a joyous meeting; the woods resounded with their joyful shouts. We have already described the return of the lost photographer to our camp, but have said nothing in regard to his personal appearance. This description is possibly unnecessary to those who have read carefully his adventure.

It is entirely natural that the reader should suppose the photographer's expression to be perfectly woe-begone, and at the same time that it should be haggard. I can assure him that even these words fail to convey any adequate idea of the poor man's personal appearance. He had certainly suffered during the last eighteen hours about as much as it is possible for any man to suffer in that brief space of time, but it had taught him a valuable lesson, one which he did not forget while we remained in Canada, and if you desire, even at this date, to hear from his own lips a sad narrative of his experience during the night that he was lost in the wilderness, it is only necessary to ask him about that night which he spent on Buck Lake.

Our party now encamped on Long Lake, spent the

time intervening between the return of the photographer and the 15th of October, was spent, very pleasantly, in deer-hunting, partridge-shooting, trout-fishing, and the taking of negatives. On the 12th of October occurred a very unexpected and memorable event in the life of the author,—his first meeting with a large bull moose face to face. It is feared though that this incident will lack pathos for our readers, as it did not result tragically for either the man or the moose. The morning of this eventful day was spent by our party in deer-hunting and fishing. Mid-day found us, however, back in our camp. Both the captain and myself remained in camp until about four o'clock, when I started out for a tramp, taking with me two bird-dogs and a shot-gun. The first part of this tramp was entirely uneventful, and the meeting which I now report did not occur until about half-past five o'clock. I was at this time walking quite rapidly down a ravine which was bounded on either side by low hills. The dogs were running a few rods ahead of me, when I was suddenly startled by a noise in the bushes, and instantly beheld, standing before me, a large bull moose within less than six rods of the muzzle of my gun.

## CHAPTER IX.

A Shot at a Bull Moose—Following the Moose Trail—Moose-calling—Breaking Camp on Long Lake—Camp on Trail between Upper Long and Sugar-Bush Lakes—Bad Weather and Consequent Delay—Preparation and Start on the Reconnoissance.

THIS animal was probably lying down when he discovered me, and the noise which attracted my attention to the spot where I saw him was probably caused by his rising. I must confess that I was taken somewhat by surprise. I realized at this instant that I was ill prepared to meet this sort of game. The bird-dogs appeared still more surprised; they stood where I first discovered them,—only about twenty feet from the king of the forest, but showed no disposition to move, and they were also silent as the grave. This position was firmly maintained by them until the animal had finally concluded to withdraw from us, and had actually started off, when the dogs promptly followed and gave tongue in great abundance, although I observed that they kept a very respectful distance from the fleeing beast. The first glance which I obtained of this huge

"The first glance which I obtained of this huge animal was while he was standing with his side towards me."

animal was while he was standing with his side towards me. I dropped instantly on my knees in order that I might more readily make search for a cartridge charged with buckshot. I thought I had some in the pocket of my hunting-coat. I drew from my pockets all my cartridges; placing them on the ground before me, after examining each separately, I discovered, to my sorrow, that all were loaded with number five shot.

What could I do? The moose was now facing me, having changed his position and advanced a few steps nearer towards me. He was now looking directly at me, and seemed to be deeply interested in what I was doing. At that moment I removed from my pocket a Winchester rifle cartridge, calibre 44, and the idea struck me, I will put this down on the bird-shot and blaze away at this animal. Prompted by this thought, I dropped a rifle cartridge into each barrel of my shot-gun and fired at the moose's head. The old king of the forest did not immediately change his position, but within a few seconds he lowered his head and shook it violently, while at the same time he stamped on the ground. It was evident that I had only succeeded in enraging the old monster. He was now acting like an infuriated bull which had been assailed by the horseman and afterwards attacked by the banderilleros in a Spanish bull-fight.

I did not stop to discuss the question, What will the moose do under these circumstances? In fact, the thought uppermost in my mind at that moment was, What shall I do? How can I kill the monster? I remembered that after firing the shot I had thoughtlessly lowered the muzzle of my gun, thus allowing the rifle-bullet to fall from the barrel which I had not yet discharged. I now began to search for another rifle cartridge. I finally found two. The thought now occurred to me, it will be prudent to reload the barrel that had been emptied. Unfortunately, I had trouble in removing the empty cartridge. While thus engaged, the animal began to move sluggishly, not directly forward, but forward and slightly to the left. He had not taken many steps when I succeeded in getting the empty cartridge out of the barrel and a loaded one into its place, then quickly the rifle cartridges were dropped on the bird-shot. This work had been performed too tardily. It is true the animal was still within sight. The gun was quickly raised, but I was unable to draw a clear bead on the fleeing monster. I waited a few seconds, hoping for a better opportunity; but finally he made his escape without my firing another shot at him. I have already said that the movements of this animal were sluggish at first, but they gradually became more rapid, and he had not travelled more than five or six rods when his antlers were thrown on his neck, and his movements had become so rapid as to make his body indistinctly visible. The most rapid movements of the animal have been described as a shambling trot, which I am convinced is correct, while its walk is not less awkward. The bird-dogs, that had remained immovable and as silent as the dead in the tombs of Egypt until the great monster had fairly started away from them, now followed in hot pursuit and gave an abundance of tongue.

The striking of the great antlers of this king of the forest against the small tree and brush, as he rapidly passed through the woods, made nearly as much noise as our discreet dogs; but these sounds were soon lost to my ears.

I do not think that either myself or the moose was ever entirely satisfied with the termination of this meeting. It is true that the moose rather reluctantly withdrew from the field after I had drawn blood, but he did not thereby yield to the demand which I had made. The bird-shot fairly peppered the poor animal's face, while the rifle cartridge went far from the mark at which it was aimed.

I now started for the lake-shore in order that I might signal the captain to come for me with a canoe and take me back to the camp, my wishes in this matter being made known to him by the firing of a prearranged signal. I took the precaution, however, in this case to break the bushes along my route to the shore, so that I might be able to return to this spot the next morning in company with my guides. The captain now made his appearance, and we returned to camp.

This day had been cloudy, and there was an occasional sprinkling of rain, whilst during the night there was a pretty heavy fall. I dreamed much during the sleeping hours of the night of moose and moose-hunting. We arose the following morning soon after daylight. It was still cloudy, but the rain had ceased. We started immediately after breakfast for the scene of my meeting with the moose. The precaution which I had taken on the previous day enabled me to readily approach the spot. We discovered this morning that an old tree standing near where the moose's head had been had received the rifle cartridge. Prior to this meeting with the moose, the question had been frequently discussed around our camp-fire whether it were practical to trail these animals without the assistance of a tracking snow. The captain had firmly maintained that it was impracticable, more especially at this particular season while the ground is covered with newly-fallen leaves, which lie very lightly on the earth-mould in which the impression of the foot is made. The captain, however, informed us that he had never attempted to follow a trail of the moose under these circumstances, but was, nevertheless, fully assured that it could not be done. The author, on the contrary, stoutly maintained that it was possible, that this fact had been repeatedly demonstrated by other sportsmen, and that it was only necessary to examine their records to prove its feasibility. The captain said in reply to this argument, "I don't believe very much in these statements made in books, but I shall test this question at the first opportunity."

Here was the opportunity, and the captain was not slow to avail himself of it. We started off on the trail, which we followed without intermission until about two o'clock in the afternoon. This trail was very circuitous. We started on it about a mile from our camp, followed it about eight miles, and were then within three hundred yards of our tent. This morning was cloudy; some rain fell, though not enough to seriously embarrass us; but the rainfall of the previous night made the trailing of the moose more difficult than it would otherwise have been. The morning's labor has demonstrated the fact, to the entire satisfaction of the captain and all the others in our party, that a moose may be quite easily trailed without the aid of a tracking snow. It is true that some difficulty is found in those cases where the trails intersect each other, where the animals have passed principally over rocky ground which is not covered with a sufficient amount of earth-mould to receive the impressions, and likewise in those cases where the earth is covered so completely with a short, thick underbrush that the animal's foot does not really come in contact with the earth.

The captain was very sceptical in regard to moose-calling, and I attempted to convince him by reading from Frank Forester's "Field Sports" the following:

"Another, and yet more fatal, method by which man

treacherously turns the poor brute's very pleasure into a lure to certain death, is to simulate the cry of the cow moose, which is easily done by immersing the lower end of a common cow-horn partially in the water of some pool or river, and blowing through it in a note very easily acquired, which perfectly resembles the lowing of the female, and which rarely or never fails to bring down the finest of the bulls from their haunts in the mountain glens, to the ambush of the lurking hunter, in search of their amorous mates. The Indians use for this purpose the bark of the beech or alder, or a postman's tin horn, and with this rude implement are perfect adepts in producing the sound requisite to call the bull to his love. The afternoon and the silence of the moonlight night are the best times for this mode of hunting, and cowardly and treacherous as it may appear, it is perhaps the most perilous and not the least exciting method of attacking these giant deer. For, in the first place, the bull moose may generally be heard roaring in the upland glens, responsive to the simulated call, long ere they reach the hunter's station, and the interval between each successive bellow, nearer and louder, and more full of passionate fury, is necessarily a moment of the keenest excitement  Then comes the tramp of his approaching gallop, the crash of branches torn asunder by his impetuous charge, and at last the presence, in the full heat and heyday of his amorous rage, of the forest champion. Again when he discovers that it is a cheat, and that no cow moose is on the spot expectant of his caresses, his fury is tremendous and appalling; for, shy and timid as is this monstrous animal at every other season, during the rutting time he is dangerous and savage in the extreme, and will even attack a man when provoked, if he cross his path in his moments of wanton dalliance.

"If he discovers then the hunter who is luring him by playing with his tenderest passions, he will charge him on the instant, fearless; and woe betide the luckless wight whose hand trembles in the aim, or whose rifle misses fire at that crisis. A bull moose seventeen or eighteen hands in height, with antlers of six feet spread, and hoof as big as an ox's, the edges of which cut like a sabre, and which he can handle as deftly as a prize-fighter, is anything but a pleasant customer at close quarters."

This statement, however, failed to carry conviction to the captain's mind, and his reply was that he had never heard this moose-calling, although he had spent much time in these forests. In answer to this statement I merely called his attention to the fact that he had only been acquainted with the moose ten or twelve years, since they were not previously found in this section of Canada; and that, *even according to his own admissions*, he had never spent any time in the moose country during their rutting season. "This is all very true," replied the captain. "I shall now keep my ears open, and if I hear these bulls bellowing, then I shall be prepared to admit the truth of the statement made in the book." He had only a short time to wait, since the next move brought us fairly into the moose country, and while we were still pushing forward on the portage, having scarcely yet reached the Sportsman's Paradise, the loud bellowing of a bull moose was distinctly heard by our whole party. The captain listened attentively to these sounds, and then exclaimed, "I am satisfied that there is no animal in these woods that can make such a noise but the old bull moose; let us now listen for the voice of the cow." The packs were quickly placed on the ground, and every ear was attentively listening for these sounds. It was not many minutes before the old bull's bass voice was distinctly heard bellowing to his inamorata, and the more modest tones of the cow were soon heard in reply. The captain instantly said, "I am convinced by my own ears, and nothing less would have ever satisfied me." These sounds were frequently heard by us during the ensuing month while we remained in the moose country, but we soon lost our interest in them, inasmuch as the question which had been raised, in regard to calling these animals, was now effectively settled.

Our departure from the camp on Long Lake took place on the 15th of October. The leaves had mostly disappeared from the deciduous trees in this wilderness, thus extending our vision, and affording us a better opportunity to "still hunt" successfully. We had awaited this condition of things with much anxiety, but a still further improvement would probably soon follow. A light tracking snow would now render most favorable the conditions for moose-hunting. The falling of the leaves had admitted light into the woods, and now a slight fall of snow, three or four inches, would enable the sportsman to noiselessly follow his game under the most favorable circumstances. The most favorable condition for still-hunting commonly follows soon after a fall of snow. During the storm the game remains inactive; but when it has ceased, the moose, deer, and other animals come out from their covers and leave their fresh imprints on the snow, where there were previously no tracks or traces. Under those circumstances no time need be lost in an examination of the track for the purpose of determining whether it be new or old; but when several days have elapsed since the fall of snow, then it remains to be determined whether the imprints are fresh before the sportsman spends much time on them. The reader will now remember that this hunt was organized especially for the purpose of hunting the moose, and, inasmuch as our guides were entirely inexperienced in the art of "calling," it therefore was necessary for us to depend entirely on trailing them. The halt on Long Lake was preparatory for the work which was to follow.

Having spent considerable time in these preparations, and also in awaiting the arrival of those conditions favorable to moose-hunting, we finally broke camp about eight o'clock on the morning of October 15. We travelled in our canoes as far as the head of Long Lake. We then crossed over the portage from this lake to Beaver Pond. The distance from Long Lake to the pond is about a mile and a half. The guides were rather slow in bringing up our luggage this morning; and, therefore, for the purpose of passing the time pleasantly, I started off into the woods, taking with me Ponto and Bummer in search of partridges. I found a number of birds about two miles from the pond, and killed two with my rifle. I then made an attempt to return to the place which I had left in the early part of the day. This was a much more difficult task than I had anticipated; but, after having wandered about some time, I finally struck the trail which I had passed over in the morning. I was now in doubt in regard to the direction which I should here take, but started off promptly, knowing full well that I should soon recognize some familiar object. I soon found myself once more on Long Lake. It was now entirely clear to my mind what must be done. It was only necessary for me to turn about and follow the trail back to Beaver Pond; which was very easily accomplished owing to the fact that the passage of our party over the same during the day had converted it into a well-marked pathway. I soon reached this pond, but a new difficulty was now encountered. The photographer and both guides had moved forward from this spot towards the next lake, taking with them all the baggage, and inasmuch as they travelled in the canoes, the trail was lost at the water's edge only a few feet from the spot where I had been in the morning, but I did not know where I would be able to pick it up again. There was no time to be lost. Darkness would soon be on us. I now determined to walk around the pond; a somewhat difficult task, owing to the marshes or swamps that surrounded it. I was fortunate in finding the trail made by our party where it left this pond, and promptly started forward on it, being happily rewarded by coming up with my friends after a brisk walk of about twenty minutes. The trail that I was now following I found to be remarkably clear, owing to the fact that it had been so recently made. The photographer and guides had halted on the portage, erected their tents, and were prepared to spend the night pleasantly.

The deer-dogs were absent from the camp this morning

when we moved out, and have not yet made their appearance. The following day was spent on the portage. The captain returned in the morning to the old camp on Long Lake, and there found the missing dogs, which he immediately brought forward. George Ross commenced at an early hour to carry forward our luggage to the next lake. The following night found us encamped on the portage leading from Upper Long Lake to Sugar-Bush Lake. I am aware of the fact that having written much of Long Lake, it is unfortunate to be compelled to write of another lake as Upper Long Lake, but this condition of things seems unavoidable, since these names are the only ones which have heretofore been applied to these bodies of water. It was eight days after our departure from the camp on Long Lake, where we had prepared our venison and made everything ready for the grand moose-hunt, before we really started out on the long-contemplated reconnoissance. This time was not, however, spent in complete idleness. The reader will remember that we started from Long Lake on the morning of the 15th of October, and that we reached our camping-ground, which is on the portage between Upper Long Lake and Sugar-Bush Lake, on the evening of the 16th, thus having consumed two days in travelling towards the moose country. This camp is situated about ten rods from Upper Long Lake and a half-mile from Sugar-Bush Lake. While the guides were clearing the ground which we had selected for our tent, they discovered a considerable number of modern Indian relics. This discovery led them to look about the spot more carefully, and a few minutes' observation was sufficient to satisfy the whole party that this ground had been occupied as an Indian camp within a few years. The most of the large trees had then disappeared, but since that time a thick underbrush had sprung up. The captain remembered that an Indian tribe had located here about ten years previously, engaged in the manufacture of maple-sugar during a single season, and then departed for parts to him unknown. It was this fact which had given the name (Sugar-Bush) to the lake that was situated about half a mile from our camp. We discovered about here many old birch-bark vessels, some of which were employed by them to receive the sap as it came from the trees, and others that had evidently been used to transport it from the trees to the spot where it was evaporated, or "boiled down," as the backwoodsmen say.

The weather during our stay in this camp, prior to taking our departure for the reconnoissance, was exceedingly changeable. One day it might rain. The next would probably give us a variety; thus, in the morning it might be cloudy, but before noon we might get rain, snow, and hail, followed by a cold night and the formation of ice. In other cases the rainfalls were accompanied with heavy thunder and followed by warm sunshine. This sort of weather was not encouraging to any party of sportsmen contemplating cutting loose from their base, leaving behind them tents and blankets, sleeping in the woods without shelter, and all this exposure and hardship merely for the love of the chase. Furthermore, the reader should at this point fully understand that even now we are having very fine sport. Since our arrival here we have killed many deer, have taken many trout, and the photographer has kept our larder amply supplied with ruffed grouse. In this camp our supplies have been most plentiful, and I have been rather reluctantly compelled to think that our guides have very little anxiety to go forward; but my wishes in this matter do not harmonize with theirs. I came into this wilderness for the special purpose of hunting the moose, and I am determined to accomplish this object.

We find many moose-tracks in these woods; we have spent two days in trailing, but they have thus far eluded us. I am satisfied, in my own mind, that we are scarcely yet on the border of the Sportsman's Paradise. That there is such a place I am not prepared to deny; but the all-important question at this moment is, How shall I now reach it? It is feared that the reader, at this moment, is ready to assert that my faith is not well founded. I must, therefore, ask him to keep silence for the time being, while I assure him that I have studied this question very carefully since my arrival in Canada, and have still an abundance of faith. Let the reader carefully review with me the ground-work of my faith before he follows me on my reconnoissance, because I wish him to become an enthusiast, in order that he may enjoy this moose-hunt as I enjoyed it. Therefore I will here confide to him the fact that, prior to my departure for Canada in 1884, I had positively learned that Captain Ross and his brother, Wellington, had already killed several moose in this country. The exact number I had not yet learned. After my arrival, I ascertained from the captain that he had killed ten and his brother had killed a somewhat smaller number. I now endeavored to locate the place where these successes had occurred, and, at the same time, to fix the limit or the extreme range of the moose. Both the captain and Wellington agreed that their successful moose-hunts had taken place near the divide of the water-sheds of the Maganetawan and Ottawa Rivers, about twenty-five miles west of the source of the Petarwawa River. They were united in asserting that they had killed their moose within a space of less than two miles square, but they supposed that the moose ranged over a space in this forest seventy-five miles square. Wellington supposed the centre of the moose region to be near the source of the Petarwawa River, and he was inclined to urge us forward to that point as the most desirable spot to commence our hunt.

The captain, however, opposed this suggestion on the grounds that it would be almost impossible to transport, from a point so distant, our trophies. It was also apparent to me that, inasmuch as neither of my guides had ever been in the Petarwawa country, it would probably be better to keep on the ground with which the captain was already familiar. The question which I raised in the early part of my sojourn in the woods, during this hunt, was, How shall we most advantageously locate the whereabouts of moose in the greatest abundance? The fact was recognized by all our party that the moose might be found scattered over a very large portion of this territory, but it was also unquestionably true that in certain districts they would be found in large numbers. I had carefully discussed, with the captain and his brother, the most practical method of starting a moose-hunt, and had suggested to them the plan which was finally adopted, and designated by us as a reconnoissance.

This plan, as adopted, required the consideration of two very important subjects. It had been determined that the reconnoissance should include the making of a circuit of eighty or one hundred miles. The performance of this task would require about four or five days. We have already considered some of the questions pertaining to the locality of the hunt, and have finally determined that our circuit shall embrace the ground which has already been so successfully hunted over by the captain and his brother.

The next important question demanding our consideration is, Where shall we abandon our tents and luggage? The point selected for this purpose must be such as will recommend it on account of its proximity to the ground on which the hunt is to be made, while it is likewise highly important that it should not be too far removed from some point which is accessible to an ox-team and jumper, inasmuch as the lakes and rivers will be frozen over before our hunt is ended, and thus closed against our canoes. These questions were all carefully discussed, and the captain's thorough knowledge of the country enabled him to determine for us all these highly-important points. He assured me that our tents and other luggage could be brought to a point about five miles distant from the nearest settler's cabin, and there, he thought, we could obtain the services of the ox-team and jumper. It should be remembered, however, by our readers who are unacquainted with these grand forests, that some sort of a road must exist in order to make the ox-team and jumper available in these cases. The captain informed us that the road which now terminated at the settler's cabin was only available for this sort of travel; and we therefore determined to move our camp from its present location forward to Camp Lake, where we would be only about five miles from Mr. Harkness's clearings, the nearest pioneer settler. This movement was finally postponed until after the reconnoissance, for the reason that it was thought barely possible that our discovery of moose in some unexpected part of the forest might render some other base more desirable. The arrangements for this reconnoissance contemplated the maintenance of camp in our rear, where the trophies of the hunt, the photographer's instruments, and other luggage could remain safely in the care of Mildenberger, while the captain, George Ross, and myself were making our tour through this grand forest for the purpose of determining the exact locality where the moose were to be found in the greatest abundance. It therefore became necessary for the guides, before our start, to prepare the wood for Mr. Mildenberger (inasmuch as he had not yet become expert in the use of the axe) which would enable him to keep the fire burning during our absence. It was also thought necessary to take enough bread to serve the whole party through the entire reconnoissance. Attempts at these preparatory efforts were often made last week, but in every instance the work was interrupted by a storm. The weather has been very unfavorable. Storm after storm has interfered with our plans. I am now tired of and impatient with these delays. I must soon push forward the reconnoissance and thus put an end to this anxiety and doubt, whether the weather becomes more favorable or not, as I can no longer endure this suspense. Deer-hunting has already become monotonous to me, and I am determined to seek in this grand forest larger game, other scenery, and new excitement in the chase.

I am told by the captain that the exposure and fatigue inseparable from moose-stalking is so great as to deter many of the pioneer backwoodsmen from attempting to participate in it. He pictures for me the discomforts that may arise from a severe storm at this season of the year, when we are separated from our tents and blankets, and thus compelled to endure its merciless peltings after a long and weary day's tramp. He reminds me of the fact that when I first came into the Canadian forest, only a few years since, I was scarcely able to endure the hardships of an ordinary deer-hunt, and then asks me, *Can you now tramp forty miles in a day, sleep on the frozen ground at night, and repeat this effort for several days continuously?* He likewise kindly suggested that he, accompanied by George Ross, could make this reconnoissance while I remained in the camp with the photographer, and thus avoided the hardships attendant on the discovery of the most favorable locality for moose-hunting. It should here be remembered by our readers that it was now, at this time, our intention to discover the whereabouts of the game which we sought, rather than to kill the same.

This proposition was rejected by the author, since it did not harmonize with his wishes. He desired greater activity, new sports, and changed surroundings.

The 23d day of October had been reached; our party was still encamped on the portage between Upper Long and Sugar-Bush Lakes; the preceding night had been cold and rainy, the morning was cold and cloudy, with occasional gusts of wind accompanied by falls of snow and hail. This damp, cold atmosphere is productive of a chilly, disagreeable sensation which seems to permeate every part of our bodies while we stand listlessly about our camp-fire. These disagreeable sensations, coupled with autumn's grave and cheerless surroundings, have caused me to think this morning of my fireside and family. The leafless trees, sombre clouds, angry gusts of wind, and the pelting storms do not commonly produce in me the most agreeable mental conditions, but that morning I was especially gloomy. It was therefore necessary that I should make some effort to arouse myself from this horrible condition of despondency. I could not bear the thought of remaining one day longer inactive in camp. It was therefore necessary that we should start immediately on our long-premeditated reconnoissance, *and start we did*, although the weather was most unpromising. The announcement to my guides that we would make ready and leave our camp as soon as possible was, I presume, owing to the unsettled state of the weather, somewhat of a surprise; however, but little preparation was now required, and before nine o'clock we took our departure from camp. We started off in the direction of Sugar-Bush Lake, and discovered a fresh moose-trail within three hundred yards of our tent. These imprints of the animal's feet left in the soft earth were so clear that we were entirely satisfied as to his identity, and it was equally certain that this traveller had crossed at this point during the previous night, since there were no tracks at this place during the preceding day. The tracks indicated that the animal had passed leisurely within a few rods of our tents while we were probably sleeping, and near us there were at that moment five dogs. This is the second moose which has come within close proximity to us during the night since we reached the Lower Long Lake. Having spent a few moments in the examination of this trail, we then started forward and soon reached Sugar-Bush Lake, where we entered our canoes, paddled across, and were soon tramping once more in the forest. Hail and rain, with fitful gusts of wind, now alternated with each other, but my body was warmed with the exercise and my spirits buoyed up in anticipation of the grand and exciting chase on which we expected so soon to enter. Sunshine was no longer necessary for my happiness, and the "blue devils" which made time hang so heavily on my hands in the morning had now been driven off.

Our route this morning took us through a heavily-wooded and somewhat hilly country, although our progress was not much impeded by underbrush, and this, in fact, is generally true of the great forest in which we are now journeying, except where we are so unfortunate as to enter its swamps and low ground. We have, heretofore, travelled through this forest in our canoes, keeping on the lakes and rivers as long as this was practicable, endeavoring to avoid, so far as possible, long portages, but the country in which we are now about making our reconnoissance is not so well adapted to this mode of travel.

The lakes are less numerous and the portages are longer; and, furthermore, we could not, in this way, accomplish the object of this movement, since we would not be brought into contact with the evidences of the presence of moose, which are generally found only in the forest.

The canoes we therefore abandoned on Sugar-Bush Lake, and we now endeavored to follow the ridges and high ground as much as possible. The captain is carrying, this morning, a tomahawk, one tin cup, one coffee- or tea-kettle, one rubber blanket, one single woollen blanket, a small quantity of dried venison, bread, coffee, tea, and salt. The reader will now observe that we have abandoned nearly all our camp luggage, that we are not even supplied with knives and forks, and possess only a single cup from which to drink our coffee, although there are three persons in the party. The captain estimates the weight of his pack at fifteen pounds, and, therefore, may be regarded as in light marching trim. He walked in front of the party, George Ross and myself following behind, sometimes in true Indian file, while at others we fell into position on the right and left flanks. The captain's advance was at all times noiseless, while his keen and practised eye penetrated into every nook and corner. He likewise listened to every sound, and instantly recognized the voice of every bird and beast of the forest. The long and active experience which he has had in the Canadian forests has made him an expert in all matters pertaining to woodcraft, trapping, and hunting. The morning's journey passed without the occurrence of any incident worthy of narration. At one o'clock we halted on a high ridge, which, at this moment, was whitened with snow, and started a small fire in order to prepare some coffee. A few moments after this halt was made, George Ross discovered a partridge standing on the ground about thirty yards from him. He raised his Winchester rifle and fired two shots at the bird's head. I then called to this guide to stop shooting at the bird and give the captain and myself a chance. This he readily consented to do, and then we took our two shots, but still the bird remained unharmed, and finally concluded to fly off without causing the waste of more ammunition. This failure to kill our game must be explained, I think, by the extreme politeness of the bird, which continued to render obeisance to us by unceasingly bowing its head from the moment when it was first discovered until it flew away.

Lest the reader should, however, find himself inclined to think that the failure was simply due to a want of skill, which he may now imagine that he possesses, I will here only venture to suggest that, when an opportunity offers, he, too, should try, as an experiment, to decapitate, with a rifle, an exceedingly polite partridge while it is constantly bowing its head.

## CHAPTER X.

THE FIRST DINNER—KILLED A DEER—FOLLOWING A MOOSE-TRAIL—CAMPED ON THE TRAIL—PREPARATION FOR SPENDING THE NIGHT—OUR LEAN-TO—A SNOW-STORM—LONG, DREARY TRAMP—DISCOVERY OF A MOOSE-YARD—A HIGHLY-EXCITING CHASE—KILLED TWO RED DEER—A DISGUSTED AND ANGRY CAPTAIN—HONEST TOIL BRINGS REFRESHING SLEEP—THE HUNT RESUMED.

COFFEE having been prepared, the captain opened his pack, drew from it some dried venison and cramper, a preparation which is sometimes by courtesy called bread, and then proceeded to distribute these articles to the party. He then filled the tin cup with hot coffee, passed the same to me, and when I had taken a drink of this delicious beverage I returned it to him, and he proceeded to quench his thirst, and then passed the cup to George Ross. In this manner the cup was kept circulating, and we were thus supplied with our coffee. The captain was the only individual in our party supplied with a hunting-knife. George Ross and myself were, however, provided with rather small pocket-knives; it will therefore be readily seen that the captain was able to make the rough sections of dried venison and cramper with his knife, while we could with our own implements make the necessary subdivisions, and thus prepare our food for mastication. Neither forks nor plates had been provided for this reconnoissance; fingers taking the place of the former article, while a chip from a neighboring tree, or a suitable piece of birch-bark, served as a very good substitute for the latter. The earth, which we commonly employed as a table, and which we likewise used in lieu of camp-stools or chairs when taking our meals, was now covered with snow, and consequently we remained standing while taking this mid-day meal.

Ample justice having been done to the coffee, dried venison, and cramper, and without waiting for dessert, finger-bowl, or cigars, we moved forward. We had proceeded about one mile from the spot where the halt had been made for our dinner when the captain, who was leading the party, being only a few yards in advance of George Ross and myself, raised his right hand as a signal for us to come to a stand-still; but he soon after beckoned us to come forward to the spot where he stood. He had, at the moment when he gave the signal to stop, just reached a point near the top of a ridge, which we were ascending, that enabled him to overlook this eminence and obtain a view of another ridge, distant about one hundred and fifty yards. The instant he gave this signal it was plain to both George and myself that he had sighted game. His manner at such times was always characteristic, and could not be misinterpreted by those who were familiar with him. The instant he sighted game he would throw up his right hand and then remain as motionless as a marble statue, unless he desired to bring either George or myself to his side; but the second signal was sure to follow the first during this reconnoissance, since the captain did not carry a gun.

Promptly after the second signal was given, in this instance, both George and myself were at the captain's side. He now whispered in my ear, "There stands a fine buck on the next ridge; what shall we do, kill him or not?" Prior to our departure from the old camp this morning I had told the captain that I preferred not to kill game, except one bull moose, the head of which I desired as a souvenir, unless the flesh could be used as food; hence this conversation, in which the captain urged the slaughter, and I rather reluctantly consented to it. Already the novelty of deer-shooting had worn off with me, having been in the woods now more than a month, and I therefore found myself strongly disinclined to continue the slaughter except to keep up the food-supply.

The captain's next inquiry was, "Will you take the shot or shall George have it?" My answer was in favor of George, who now dropped quietly on his knee, drew a fine bead on the animal, which was at this moment slowly walking along the ridge, and within a few seconds pulled the trigger which sent the leaden pill from his trusty Winchester rifle into the side of the beautiful creature, which had not yet either scented or seen danger. The instant the white puff of smoke was seen to issue from the muzzle of the gun the *deer leaped high in the air and bolted forward with the speed of the wind*, the motion of the animal being now so rapid as to render his form indistinctly visible, but after thus running about five hundred yards its movements became perceptibly slower, more irregular, and it was evident that the bullet had struck a vital part. A moment later the captain shouted, "He has fallen!" quickly afterwards, "He is up again!" but scarcely had these sounds passed away when the deer passed over a ridge and was thus lost to view. We started promptly forward to the spot where the animal had been seen to fall; there we found the ground covered with blood, and from this point we could easily follow him by the bloody trail. He was finally found dead on the slope of a hillock only a few yards from the spot where he had been last seen.

It took the captain but a few moments to remove the skin and cut from the carcass a choice piece of venison sufficient for our supper and breakfast, when we were again off on the tramp.

The storm had now ceased, a little later a bright sunshine had lighted up our pathway through the woods, the snow which covered the fallen leaves rapidly disappeared, while the fitful gusts of wind which prevailed in the morning were entirely absent in the evening. The morning and the early part of the afternoon had passed without the discovery of any fresh moose signs, but our search was rewarded later in the day, when we struck a very promising trail. The herd consisted of three animals, presumed to be one bull and two cows, but I think there is a certain amount of uncertainty in the prognosticating of the sex, since it is entirely based on the size of the track made by the animal. We discovered that these animals had been browsing near the point where we struck their trail, and furthermore, the tracks had evidently been made since the snow had melted off. Both these discoveries were very encouraging, since the moose commonly lies down after eating, and consequently the hunter reasonably expects to find him within a short distance of the last feeding-ground, while in this instance the snow had disappeared within the hour preceding our arrival on the trail.

The captain having familiarized himself with all these peculiarities of the trail, speedily and forcibly enjoined upon us the necessity of moving forward with the greatest degree of caution, lest by a careless step a noise might be made which would frighten away the game that we now sought. We are now in a high state of excitement. *The grandest game in the Canadian forest is now almost within our reach. Our hearts are beating strongly;* hope buoys us up; the long tramp of the day is forgotten; we feel no fatigue and fear no failure. The captain creeps along through the brush, over the fallen trees, over the rotten twigs, which are frequently so well hidden by fallen leaves as to be wholly imperceptible, but there is no sound produced by his movements. He trails game as cautiously as the cat follows the mouse. The sportsman who attempts to follow him should keep well in his rear, but within easy hearing distance, so that in the first instance the game may not be frightened by a mis-step, and secondly that he may be able to come quickly into position when shooting is to be done.

Having spent about two hours on this moose-trail, which was at first very circuitous, but which finally lost much of this peculiarity, we were reluctantly compelled to halt in order to make the necessary preparations for spending the night; we therefore encamped on this trail, with the intention of following it up in the morning. The first thing done was the selection of a suitable spot on which to erect our lean-to. The place selected for this purpose was by the side of the body of an old fallen tree, where the ground was favorable for our bed,—free from stone, etc. The body of this tree formed a wall, which was about two feet high, for the lean-to; and, inasmuch as it rested firmly on the ground at this point, effectually kept out the wind on this side of it. The next thing done was the preparation of four poles, employed to support the roof, which consisted of a rubber cloth, the dimensions of which were about five by seven feet. The poles were about ten feet in length, with a diameter at the base of two and a half inches and something less than one inch at the top. The poles, properly sharpened at the base, were driven into the ground on the side of the trunk of the fallen tree opposite to the one on which we intended to make our bed, and the distance was so chosen that when these supports rested on this wall, which served as a fulcrum, or prop, the anterior portion of our roof was raised about four feet above the ground. The rubber cover was then placed over these poles and made fast by the use of shoe-strings, that we had brought with us, after which the ends of our habitation were closed by evergreen boughs, selected for this purpose. It will now be seen by the reader that the lean-to has been so constructed as to close the sides of it against the wind, and that only the front remains open, before which there is placed a fire, which is kept burning during the whole night, and which may be easily so managed as to supply the requisite amount of heat. It was still necessary to provide wood for the fire and balsam twigs for the bed. This was promptly done, the wood being placed in such a position as to occasion little inconvenience to put it on the fire when it was required, while the twigs were arranged in the most approved style for the bed. The next order of business consisted in the preparation of the evening meal, which was composed of venison, coffee, and bread. The fresh venison was cut into suitable pieces and then roasted on the spits over our fire, while the coffee was prepared in the usual manner. The fresh deer-skin was brought into use as a partial cover (although the only one we possessed) for the balsam twigs composing our bed. Having completed our evening meal, we then took such positions about the fire as enabled us to dry our clothing, after which we made ready to retire by simply removing our boots, which is done as a precautionary act to prevent the destruction of the same by fire. The balance of the wardrobe is retained on our bodies as an additional protection against cold, since we only possess a single blanket with which to cover the whole party. The author has detailed thus minutely the preparations made for spending the first night while we were out on our reconnoissance, and this will answer for the succeeding ones while we were thus engaged.

I suffered somewhat from the cold during the night, especially my feet, but my body was pretty well protected by sleeping between the captain and George Ross. The first part of the night was comparatively warm, but before the dawn of day it became very cold, and ice formed nearly or quite an inch thick on the little pools of water near us.

Thus terminates the record of the first day spent on

our reconnoissance, while the second begins with the following entries:

*Friday, October* 24.—We encamped last night on the moose-trail, but it is obliterated this morning by a slight fall of snow. The leaves were wet last evening, but are firmly frozen now; consequently the slightest movement in walking is attended with a degree of noise entirely incompatible with success in still-hunting. There is no possibility of our killing game until we are able to move about more quietly. The storm continues,—fine, hard flakes of snow, closely allied to hail, are falling about us, and producing considerable noise by coming in contact with the frozen leaves and various parts of the forest-trees. The morning was dark and gloomy, but we started off on our tramp soon after daylight, having eaten our breakfast while it was yet dark.

The entire party is in good spirits, and, notwithstanding the severe and prolonged efforts made yesterday, there is no complaint of fatigue or other ill effects arising from our tramp. The author found himself somewhat annoyed, however, by the entrance of snow into all the crevices of his clothing, especially about his neck, where it was constantly melting, and the cold water gravitating downward over the various parts of his body. Under more favorable circumstances the remedy for this annoyance would have been very easy; but no man in our party is, at this time, in possession of a handkerchief, and consequently "the ills which cannot be cured must be endured."

During the whole forenoon the storm continued, and at one o'clock, when we halted for our lunch, the ground was everywhere covered to the depth of about two inches with snow. Thus far the day has passed without the occurrence of any important events. In fact, we have seen only a single deer-trail, no ruffed grouse, and only two red squirrels. The conditions for still-hunting have, however, gradually improved, until now we are able to travel without much noise. Our party is cheerful; there is no despondency, although the prospect for sport is not flattering, inasmuch as the storm causes game to remain under cover. Dinner consisted of dried venison, bread, and coffee. The last of our fresh venison was consumed at breakfast this morning. The midday meal was partaken of in the same manner as that already described in connection with the first day's tramp, and consequently it need not be more fully detailed here. The start was made promptly after the completion of this repast, inasmuch as we were less comfortable while standing than when walking.

We have walked rapidly since our start to-day, have not turned aside for any purpose, and are off at the same pace and pushing forward in the same direction. About two o'clock in the afternoon we altered our general course from northeast to west, and continued in the latter direction until nearly three o'clock, when we struck a fresh moose-trail. Here began the most exciting chase it has ever been my good fortune to participate in, one in which our party saw not less than twenty moose, fired probably thirty shots, killed two red deer, but absolutely failed with the larger game. The following of the moose-trail, which we first discovered this afternoon, led us within twenty minutes into a large moose-yard, where the tracks of these animals were as numerous as the tracks of cows about a large dairy-barn soon after the first fall of snow in autumn. Here was probably about one acre of this forest which had been so thoroughly tracked over within an hour that it was wholly impossible to follow out the trail of any particular animal, on account of the numerous intersections and obliterations caused by the wanderings of this numerous herd.

Slowly, cautiously, and stealthily the captain moves over this yard. He discovers every bush which has been cropped, every tree that has been peeled, and does not even neglect to examine the evacuations: these he finds are still warm. George Ross and myself follow closely behind the captain. Our anticipations are now of the most delightful sort; the gods are favoring us; the storm ceased just before we discovered the moose-trail, and now the conditions are most favorable for the chase. Nature has provided a carpet which deadens the sounds that would otherwise be made by our foot-falls; the same covering leaves the impress made by the animals' feet, while the clouded sky enables us to behold objects equally well in any direction. We had now reached on the outskirts of the yard a point where seven tracks diverged from the common centre, and this trail we had followed only a short distance when the captain turned to me, whispered in my ear, "These moose have been here within thirty minutes; follow me slowly; make no noise!" I was momentarily puzzled by the positive assertion of my guide.

How could he so positively say, "These moose have been here within half an hour?" A glance at the tracks afforded the explanation. These imprints did not contain a single flake of snow; and therefore it is evident that they have been made since the storm ceased. The captain now asked me to keep close to him, in order that I might be in a position to fire on the game the instant it was discovered. This request was cheerfully granted. The movements of the captain now became still more cautious, while George Ross and myself followed the example of our leader. *Slowly and cautiously we moved forward. Every object, whether near or distant, if within the limit of our vision, was carefully scanned.* Twenty minutes have elapsed since we discovered that this trail had been made after the storm ceased. At this instant the captain's right hand is raised. *It is a signal for those who follow him to halt and remain silent. It is obeyed with alacrity.* The captain peers steadily for a few seconds into the forest. I was standing only a few feet behind him. He beckoned me, with a slight movement of his hand, to come to his side. The request was promptly obeyed. At this instant I photographed the expression of his face, which still remains indelibly impressed on my mind. His eyes were fixed and glared intently on the game which he had just discovered. His lips were tightly closed, his teeth completely hidden. The muscles of his face were rigidly fixed, exhibiting the most *intense excitement and resolute determination.* His body was as immovable as a statue. *He now sharply whispered,* "Don't you see them? There! there! they are running!" FIRE, FIRE AT THEM!" I had not been able to get a glimpse of the herd, although they were standing huddled together not more than one hundred yards from me, until they began to move; and then it was only a few seconds until their bodies seemed like shadows flying through the woods, on account of the rapidity of their movements. The fact that the captain was the best rifle-shot in our party had been already conceded. We all recognized his ability, including both the accuracy and rapidity with which his shots were delivered. Neither was he ignorant of his prowess, or in the least averse to chaffing those who might not possess his skill; consequently I had determined, prior to our departure from our camp, near Sugar Bush Lake, that I would give him the doubtful shots and take the more certain ones. The reader should now remember that the captain is not provided with a rifle; but I now acted promptly on my conservative resolution and quickly passed him my Ballard rifle, saying, "Take the shot! Fire away!" He seized the gun and instantly fired. Another cartridge is placed in position and quickly discharged at the retreating herd. The Ballard is dropped to the ground and the captain shouted to his nephew, "Give me your Winchester!" This request was promptly complied with; the captain was now in the possession of the desired rifle with a full magazine, and instantly started on a full run after the game. Behold his rapid strides! The best Indian runner would have been distanced by him in this chase. George has caught up my rifle; we both follow at our best speed; he leads us from the start and gains on us rapidly; bang! bang! goes the captain's rifle while he is still running. He had run about eight hundred yards, when he suddenly stopped, raised his gun, and deliberately took aim, firing four shots during this halt.

The woods are full of them.

George Ross and myself arrived on the spot while the sound of the last was reverberating through the forest. We saw at this instant a bull moose, which had been standing about one hundred yards from our leader, start forward on a run. This bull had evidently belonged to the first herd that we discovered; had been prompted by curiosity to halt in order to get a better view of his pursuers; had already received the polite attention of the captain, but now triumphantly moved off. The captain was certainly greatly excited and greatly disgusted, probably because the old bull paid so little attention to the demand which he had made upon him to halt; but not a full minute elapsed after the cessation of this firing when another herd of these animals, which we had not previously seen, started up about three hundred yards to the right of the trail made by the herd that we had been following, although the latter were, at the moment of their start, slightly in the rear of the spot where we were standing. Another race now ensued, which was no less exciting than the former. The instant that the captain heard the sounds they made while rushing through the woods, he instantly dropped his pack, which he had carried during the whole of the first race, and was off in the twinkling of an eye. The course taken by these animals led us down the gentle slope of a long hill; consequently I was enabled to keep nearer to our leader, although still falling considerably in his rear.

At the base of the slope there was found a small brook, which the captain crossed in this race. Having crossed the stream, the captain threw up his hand as a signal for me to approach him more cautiously, and quickly commenced firing again. He discharged his rifle four times in rapid succession, from this point, at a full-grown cow that was standing not more than seventy-five yards from him, although partially hidden from his view by an intervening evergreen. This animal now, in entire disregard of these polite attentions, started off on a shambling trot, and was followed by George Ross, who continued to blaze away at varying intervals during a chase which was kept up for nearly a mile, when it became apparent to the pursuer that the old cow was getting the best of the race. When this animal passed beyond the reach of the captain's bullets, it is putting it very mildly to say that he was disgusted with the results. This feeling of disgust was visible in all his movements, as well as in his facial expressions. Words were not adequate to express his feelings. Having remained silent a few minutes, he suggested that we proceed to the spot where the cow was standing when he fired the shots, and make an examination of the surroundings. This was now done, but only increased his feelings of disgust; inasmuch as we failed to find the slightest trace of injury to the animal, not even a single drop of blood or a lock of hair, on the newly-fallen snow, although there was the unmistakable impress of the animal's feet in it. In this examination only a single point was settled in the affirmative, to our mutual satisfaction, viz., the captain had undoubtedly been firing at a living moose, and not at an apparition, which might have been conjured up in certain brains. Let the reader, however, here understand that the captain is not a sportsman against whom such a charge could be well maintained. His habits are above reproach; he neither drinks nor smokes, and in all things is a plain matter-of-fact person, not even given to fiction nor any sort of exaggeration. Having completed the examination of this spot, we turned slowly away from it and walked side by side, possibly about ten rods, when the captain discovered a fine buck that had been feeding within fifty yards of us. I saw this beautiful animal a few seconds later than my guide.

The captain said, "Let me now try my skill on this deer since I have failed on the moose." The rifle was then raised; the captain took an unusually long time in taking aim, but the gun was finally discharged; the buck sprang high into the air, and all was quiet once more.

The captain quickly remarked, "I killed that deer, although I have so surprisingly failed to-day with the moose." There had been considerable delay after the shooting. Our conversation, in the mean while, had not related to this buck; in fact, neither of us thought much of this affair, but we naturally conversed on the more exciting chase of the moose; consequently, when we went in search of the carcass, it was not until after much delay that we could find even the spot where the animal stood when the shot was fired. Having at first been baffled in our search, we returned to the spot where we were standing when the shot was delivered, took our directions from this point, then found the animal's tracks in the snow, but were still unable to find his body; however, when we circled around these imprints, we found the object of our search within twenty feet of the point where he had received his death wound. He had made but a single leap and fallen dead. The deer was promptly skinned, and a choice piece selected for our present wants, after which the balance of the carcass was left behind for the use of the wolves. We now retraced our steps to the point where the captain had dropped his pack, when he started on the second moose chase. Here George Ross joined us and reported in glowing terms the incidents of his race, and the various causes of its failure. He regretted that his feet were not encased in moccasins instead of the heavy boots that he was then wearing, and assured us with much confidence that, had he been thus attired, he should certainly have provided himself with a hairy overcoat, which the old cow would now probably continue to wear, instead of himself, during the coming winter.

This young man talked wildly about the overcoat which he had barely failed to secure, and romanced nearly every day on this subject as long as he remained in the woods with us. The storm now recommenced,—snow falling once more,—night was approaching; the lean-to must be put up, wood and boughs gathered, and our frugal meal prepared. The captain desired to take one more look for game before darkness covered the earth. He was not satisfied with the results of his shooting during the afternoon. He wished to make an effort immediately, to redeem his good name; consequently, after having urged George and your humble servant to make the necessary preparation for the night, he sallied forth once more in quest of moose.

He had not expressed, either to George or myself, his

wishes on this subject, but his manner indicated plainly the thoughts which were uppermost,—even the desires of his heart. Both George and myself set about the performance of the task that had been assigned to us. This labor was agreeable,—better far than standing still in the wild storm and allowing ourselves to be buried beneath the falling snow.

One hour of brisk activity found us prepared for the evening meal and awaiting the captain's return. The twilight of the evening had gathered around us, when we heard the captain's rifle discharged twice,—the second shot following the first so quickly that George had been unable to complete the exclamation, "He is after them again," before he was interrupted by the second sound. The question now raised by George was, "What has the captain killed?" It was thought probable that the firing had been occasioned by the discovery of a moose, since these animals were certainly more numerous on this ground than the red deer; but it was not by any means certain that the captain had killed one of the kings of the forest.

It was nearly half an hour after these shots were heard when the captain returned to our camp-fire. His face was livid with rage and he stormed like a sailor, but no words of profanity passed his lips. Neither George nor myself ventured to attempt any sort of conversation with him, and he rattled on wildly,—"I will never hunt moose again! If these guns were my property I would break them over the nearest tree and start for home to-morrow morning!" On, still on, he went! After the storm had raged in all its fury for half an hour he cooled off slightly, and then narrated to us occurrences which had taken place after his separation from us. He said, "I discovered, very soon after leaving you, another herd of moose, in which there were two large bulls; succeeded in getting within fifty yards of one of these animals, which was standing with his head towards me; no other part of his body being visible at this time. I was unwilling to fire at the forehead lest the ball should glance from the bone without doing any signal service. I determined, therefore, to wait a more favorable opportunity when the game moved from its present cover,—hoping he would then present for my shot a more vulnerable part of his body. I had not long to wait when the movement was made; but, to my great disgust, the moose so turned as to become immediately and entirely invisible to me, and I could not again secure a glimpse of this fleeing animal; in the mean while, all the other members of this herd had made their escape." The captain here added, "Was not this luck enough to make a saint swear?" The interrogatory which immediately followed was, "What did you shoot at?" "I had started to come in when an old buck jumped up before me. I fired at him; the first shot broke his leg, and the second brought him to a full halt. It was then nearly dark and I did not stop to skin him, but will attend to that in the morning."

Thus ended the day's chase, and as supper was now ready, we proceeded to refresh ourselves as the next order of business. The performance of this labor produced a most salutary effect on our worthy captain. The angry expression I had observed on his face immediately after his return to our camp-fire had now been replaced with a pleasant smile. The terrible blizzard had passed away, and instead of the raging storm we now had sunshine. It was now perfectly safe to chaff the captain on his want of success,—a pastime that he greatly enjoyed, when it was done at some other person's expense,—and it should, likewise, be acknowledged that he had always previously patiently submitted to this treatment when we were so fortunate as to have an opportunity to make the application. Such an excellent opportunity to cancel the old score had never before offered since I had been in our leader's company.

I now ventured to suggest to the captain that he was a dead shot whenever he drew a bead on a bird or deer, but he was not so sure of his game when he sought to kill a moose. The captain willingly admitted that the results of the chase during the day seemed to justify my conclusion; and furthermore assured me that he would do no more moose-shooting while he was accompanied by George Ross and myself, but leave that part of the sport to us.

The evening was spent pleasantly under our lean-to, while a grand wood fire burned in front of it, although the snow continued to fall and was driven by the wind into every part of our imperfect shelter. We passed the night comfortably,—slept soundly, were thoroughly refreshed, and made ready for work the next morning. The earliest dawn of day found us busied with the preparation of the morning meal. The ground was now covered with snow to the depth of nearly five inches, although the prevailing wind had kept it from collecting upon the trees.

We have determined to spend the morning in search of moose in the vicinity where we discovered them yesterday. The captain thinks it probable that there may still be some herds which have remained undisturbed on these feeding-grounds. The whole forenoon was spent without sighting the object which we sought. It was scarcely light this morning when we started from our camp. The captain led us promptly to the spot where he had shot the old buck on the previous evening. We found him buried beneath the snow, and quickly removed his skin, which was added to the captain's pack. We then proceeded to search diligently for moose,—found a single trail,—followed it about two miles, having started him from his bed during the tramp; but, inasmuch as the wind was unfavorable, he scented us from afar and was off without affording us even a momentary glance at his lordship's person. The storm had ceased before we left the camp this morning, although it was still cloudy, but the sun came out towards noon without producing any visible effect upon the snow, since it was yet cold. We returned to the camp where we had spent the previous night soon after twelve o'clock, prepared our dinner; discovered that our bread and coffee were exhausted, and therefore decided to start immediately for our camp near Sugar-Bush Lake. The captain thought we might succeed in reaching this point some time during the forenoon of the next day. It was with feelings of despondency that we moved away from the scenes of our recent chase, that had afforded us much pleasurable excitement, although we had failed to secure the coveted prize.

## CHAPTER XI.

THE DISCOVERY OF MOOSE—THE KILLING OF TWO MOOSE AND THE WOUNDING OF ANOTHER—OUR CAMP ON MOOSE HILL—THE RETURN TO SUGAR-BUSH LAKE—A SEVERE RAIN-STORM—RETURN TO MOOSE HILL—THE DEAD MOOSE PHOTOGRAPHED—ANOTHER EXPEDITION—THE BEAR—A SNOW-STORM—A HARD TRAMP.

IT was now thought impossible that we should find another opportunity to engage in a moose-chase during this reconnoissance, and consequently we began to look about us for smaller game. We arrived at Trout Lake about half-past two o'clock; discovered a flock of ducks; fired several shots at them, and then started to walk around this body of water, which was surrounded by a cranberry marsh, but had proceeded only a few rods when the captain, who was in advance, discovered a fresh moose-track. It was finally determined, after a brief consultation, to follow this trail a short distance, in order to determine the prospect of success, while our further movements would depend entirely on the result of this investigation. Consequently the captain threw down his pack and took the lead in this movement. The trail led directly from the lake into a cedar swamp which bordered on the cranberry marsh. This swamp was filled with fallen trees, a dense underbrush, and stagnant pools of water.  We had not followed the trail more than twenty rods when it was discovered that the old bull moose had been joined by two cows, and the trio had been very recently feeding in the swamp.  The captain was much elated by this discovery, and confidently expressed the opinion that these animals would be discovered lying down near the spot where the browsing had taken place.  Our leader was in high spirits; rapidly and noiselessly passed over all obstructions; sighted and carefully examined every object in the neighborhood of the trail which we were following.

He soon emerged from the swamp and commenced the ascent of a hill where there were fewer obstructions to our progress, but prior to his reaching this point the author of these pages had fallen about six or seven rods to the rear of the leader, although George Ross had succeeded in keeping somewhat nearer.

The captain's advance is now much more cautious; he evidently expects to find the moose on this high ground. He takes a few steps forward, then halts, carefully surveys every object within the range of his vision, and has thus approached within about seventy-five or eighty yards of the summit of the hill which we are climbing.  He has suddenly halted again, and at the same instant thrown out his right hand as a signal to his followers to be more cautious in their movements.  George Ross has cautiously moved forward to his side; but the gaze of our leader has remained steadily fixed on some object in the immediate front.  He stands as immovable as the trunks of the great forest-trees with which we are surrounded.  *Behold him!*

*he is now whispering to his nephew! I know he has sighted game. A moment later he beckoned to me to come forward; repeats this signal two or three times before I reached his side. In the mean time young Ross has raised his rifle and stands with it raised in readiness for instantaneous action.* I reached the captain's side; he seized my arm and drew me about ten feet to the left of George Ross; had not yet spoken a word; but now whispered, "See that moose standing behind the underbrush? Fire at him!" Before I had time to raise my rifle George Ross had fired his first shot. The object which had been pointed out to me by the captain as a moose was almost completely hidden by the underbrush, only a small portion of the animal's flank being visible. The aim was taken at this part; the shot was fired; the animal now quickly changed his position and presented to me his rump. The captain was standing at my side; the instant the first shot was fired he shoved another cartridge into my rifle; I dropped quickly on my knee, took very deliberate aim, and forwarded my compliments once more. The animal at which this shot was fired now disappeared before I had sufficient time to reload my rifle.

I now ran a few feet to the right of George Ross, who had remained stationary and continued to shoot rapidly. From this new position I caught sight of another moose, and fired another shot. Game was no longer visible from the spot where we were standing, and consequently we started up the hill at our best speed. A few seconds later our entire party was standing about the dead cow, on which George Ross had expended his fusillade. She had

"Fire at him!"

never moved from the spot where she was standing when young Ross fired his first shot; when unable to stand longer she fell on the opposite side of a log and was thus lost to his view. The captain glanced momentarily at the dead animal, raised his head to survey the surroundings, discovered the old bull which I had mortally wounded, and instantly exclaimed, "See the old monster!" This was the signal for a new start; our party rushed forward until we were within about twelve feet of this animal's head, which he now lowered, and at the same time uttered a low bellow that greatly resembled the angry threatenings of an enraged bull. The captain instantly caught hold of my arm, as if to keep me from danger, but I scarcely think this precaution was necessary, since I had already observed the angry warnings given by the old forest king.

The captain having warned me of the danger, now leaped into the air, danced like a school-boy, seized me by the hand, offered his congratulations, while his face was wreathed in joyous smiles.

The scenes enacted here reminded me of those which I had witnessed many years ago on the battle-fields during the war of the Rebellion, when the staid generals became boys once more after gaining important victories. Well do I still remember the many manifestations of joy which followed Sheridan's victory at Cedar Creek, Virginia. Generals Sheridan, Custer, Torbert, and many other gallant officers in the Federal army were boys that day, when they learned the extent of their victory. It is hoped that the reader will pardon this wide digression from our subject and return with me to the summit of the hill in that grand forest, where these moose were slain, since a careful description of the scenes enacted here will not fail to interest any sportsman.

Already the shooting has been described which occurred on the slope of this hill while the moose were standing on its summit; and there remains little to be said of the old cow, since life was extinct before we reached the spot where she fell. The bull, when discovered, was about four or five rods distant from the point where the cow had fallen. He was at this moment standing on his forefeet, dragging his hind limbs along on the ground, endeavoring occasionally to get once more into the natural standing position, but all these efforts were fruitless. The poor animal had been paralyzed by the ball that had been fired at his rump, and passed upward, wounding the spinal cord in the lumbar region. The appearance of the old bull was not only pitiful but likewise savage at this moment. He was so severely wounded that he could not escape from his enemies, or even make that defence which his gigantic proportions declared him fitted for under more favorable circumstances. The size of the animal may be inferred from the fact that he was found to measure between the top of his shoulders and the bottom of his hoofs seventy-eight and one-half inches, while his symmetrical antlers showed a spread of nearly six feet. We viewed this noble beast while he was yet alive; the hair on his whole body was standing erect, thus naturally increasing the apparent size of the animal and likewise giving to him a more savage aspect. The long, erect hair, covering the top of the shoulders, increased the seeming height of the moose at least six or eight inches; and the same remark is equally applicable, except in degree, to the other parts of the body. The wild boar, in his own forest garb, could not present a more frightful appearance than did the king of the Canadian wilderness at this moment. It is true that this bull could not present the same formidable tusks, but his great antlers and magnificent proportions more than compensated for all that was wanting. Notwithstanding the fact that he was so severely wounded as to be able to make but very little progress in his efforts to escape, still our party remained at a very respectful distance from his antlers. Our first attention having been given to the personal appearance of this animal, our succeeding thoughts were directed to the relief of his sufferings, and for this purpose I sent a ball through him a few inches behind his shoulders. This last shot produced no marked effect; therefore I quickly fired another shot a little behind the base of his skull, which fractured the upper portion of the vertebral column and likewise wounded the medulla oblongata, which injury was followed by instantaneous death. The captain proceeded to disembowel the animals we had killed; and while thus engaged discovered that another cow had been wounded by our shots, but had succeeded in getting away. His quick eye promptly detected three fresh beds in the newly-fallen snow, and likewise that the trail from two of them led to the dead animals, which were now lying only a few yards from the same, while the other led away from the scene of action. The latter trail was well marked by the blood-stains left by the fleeing animal. It was instantly decided that we should follow up this trail. The blood-stains were numerous about the bed from which the cow had so recently risen, and the white snow was found to be copiously marked during the first half-mile of the trail; but after this distance had been passed over these markings were less numerous. It was confidently thought by our guides, while we were making the first part of our journey along this trail, that we would soon find her lifeless body; but we continued our search until warned by the near approach of sunset that we ought to retrace our steps and make

The dead monarch.

the required preparation for the night. The pack, which the captain was carrying at the moment when he discovered the moose-track near Trout Lake, still remained where he had then dropped it. It was with some regrets that we started on this retrograde movement, since we still thought that another hour spent in the search would probably be rewarded by the capture of the wounded animal. Nevertheless, we were greatly cheered by the results that had already been obtained, and we now retraced our steps with light hearts and speedy action. While thus retracing our steps we were naturally led to take a retrospective view of our doings during the day. In the morning we had started from our camp in joyful anticipation of successes just about to be realized. These pleasant anticipations were the natural outgrowth of the discovery of several herds of moose in the vicinity of our camp on the previous day. We had set forth in the morning in full expectation that before noon we should be able to kill one or more moose; at one o'clock we had returned to our camp sadly disappointed by a complete failure. In the afternoon, while wearily trudging along without any seemingly reasonable expectation of discovering the prize we sought, we had fortunately struck the single trail, which being followed, soon brought us to the full realization of our most joyous anticipations. Such are the results obtained in our various pursuits in life by industrious and persevering labor, which in the end brings its reward, although the prize is frequently attained when least expected. Dame Nature is apparently an inveterate coquette, who must be industriously and perseveringly courted for a long time, when she will turn, at some unexpected moment, and most graciously receive our caresses, thus adding surprise to conquest. Before sunset we reached the scene of our recent shooting, and made the necessary preparation for the night. The pack was promptly brought to the spot, the lean-to erected, wood and balsam boughs gathered, after which the moose-meat—which constituted our entire meal—was cooked.

We no longer had either bread, tea, or coffee. Thus the sportsman may be compelled to live, but what is the odds so long as you are happy? This was certainly the most joyful night spent by us during the whole reconnoissance. We had already accomplished more than we expected when we left our camp near Sugar-Bush Lake; had not only determined the whereabouts of the moose, but had actually slain two fine animals, a male and a female.

The early part of this evening was spent in recounting the exploits of the day, and the balance of the night in refreshing slumber,—a blessing almost unknown to the drudging professional slaves of the city. We arose early the following morning, and while it was yet dark began our preparations for the return to the old camp. The dead moose were well covered with brush, in order that the wild animals might not deface them before the photographer had completed his part of the work. The moose-meat was prepared, our breakfast eaten, and we were again off on our homeward tramp. The sun soon made its appearance; the weather had moderated, and all now went merry as a marriage bell. The partridge were found to-day in great abundance and afforded us much sport. We were no longer troubled because of their excessive politeness, but they behaved in the most approved manner, and permitted us to knock off their heads with the rifle-balls without uttering the slightest murmur. We had bagged before noon a half-dozen of these fine game-birds. During the first part of the tramp we saw only a single red deer and very few traces of moose, but when within about three miles of the old camp moose-tracks were once more found to be quite numerous; however, we now spent no time in search of these animals. We reached our camp near Sugar-Bush Lake about one o'clock, October 26, and the captain promptly prepared our dinner. We had now reached our supplies; found ourselves in possession of an abundance of flour, coffee, tea, sugar, etc. Mr. Mildenberger was absent from camp when we arrived, but returned about half-past three o'clock, and was delighted to find us in possession of the tent. He immediately inquired in regard to the success of the reconnoissance, and when informed on this subject was greatly pleased. He expressed a desire to start promptly for the scene of the moose-hunt, in order that he might photograph these animals where they had fallen. It was now so late in the day that the other members of the party thought better to postpone this movement until a later period. The captain had evidently changed his mind in regard to moose-hunting during the last forty-eight hours, since he picked up the Winchester rifle very soon after our dinner and declared his intention to start off in search of the king of the forest. He was absent from our camp about three hours, when he returned and reported having seen one moose, at which he fired a shot but did not kill the animal.

The small lakes around us are completely frozen over, but the weather is rapidly moderating this afternoon. The clouds are gathering and there are other indications of a rain-storm. The following day found us confined to our tents by the pouring rain. This storm continued twenty-four hours and the snow entirely disappeared. The advance movement commenced on the morning of the 28th of October.

This change of base is made with the intention of bringing our luggage into a more favorable position for leaving the forest after the closure of the lakes and rivers with ice. Another reason prompting this action at the present time is connected with the fact that in returning to Moose Hill, where we killed the moose, we must necessarily pass Camp Lake; and therefore we have concluded to take with us all our luggage to this point, where we will erect our tent, store such articles as may not be required for the balance of our journey, chain the dogs, place within their easy reach so much food as may be required for their sustenance during our absence, and then proceed to the end of the contemplated journey, make the desired negatives, gather up the trophies and bring them back to our base, from which all future operations will be conducted.

The rain-storm ceased during the preceding night, but the morning on which the movement began was cloudy. We crossed Sugar-Bush Lake this morning in our canoes, the ice having mostly disappeared during the storm, and arrived about noon on South Lake, where we prepared and ate our dinner. The movement was resumed and continued during the entire afternoon. We reached at a late hour a nameless lake, which we then christened Ross Lake, in honor of our chief guide. The night was spent under a lean-to, there now being four occupants instead of three, as was the case during the reconnoissance. With the appearance of daylight, on the morning of October 29, we were again moving forward on the portage. We reached Camp Lake about twelve o'clock, put everything in order there, and proceeded onward to Moose Hill, where we arrived about three o'clock the same day. The photographer proceeded immediately to make the desired negatives, while the guides were busied with the necessary preparation for the night,—skinning the moose, etc.

It had been our intention to send a guide to the nearest settler, distant from this spot fourteen miles, in order that he might remove the meat and use it for food; but our intention in this respect was frustrated by the discovery that it was already tainted by commencing decomposition.

We remained overnight at Moose Hill, and returned to Camp Lake the next day, where we arrived about four o'clock in the afternoon, having brought with us the trophies of the last hunt. We were welcomed to this camp by a canine chorus, in which the voices of our five dogs were joyously commingled, while, at the moment of our approach, they leaped gleefully about us, and added to the other manifestations of joy such caresses as they were allowed to bestow.

In acknowledgment of this kindly reception they were promptly unchained and permitted the freedom of the camp. These dumb animals have now been our constant companions for several weeks in this grand forest; have shared with us in the excitement of the chase; have aided us in securing subsistence; while we have in return for these services most willingly shared with them our food. None can appreciate the companionship and assistance rendered by hunting-dogs better than the sportsmen who have cut loose from their base of supplies and sojourn for weeks in the forest of Canada. Even the circumstances which bound together the unfortunate "Rip Van Winkle" and his dog "Snyder" are not more favorable for this development.

The day following our return to Camp Lake was stormy; the falling rain kept us close to our tent, although we attempted a deer-hunt in the afternoon, which ended unsuccessfully, inasmuch as one of our dogs strayed away and was not recovered while we remained in this forest; neither did we obtain a deer. The next morning, November 1, the captain announced that a deer was required for our larder, and requested George Ross and myself to proceed to Cedar Lake, distant from our camp less than one mile, taking with us a canoe, in order that we might watch on this body of water while he would endeavor to start our remaining deer-dog at such a point as to drive the game to us. The plan thus sketched was successfully carried out, and before noon we had a fine buck in our camp. Mr. Mildenberger, the photographer, has for several weeks assumed the responsibility of keeping the camp supplied with ruffed grouse, and it has never been found necessary to give him any aid in the performance of this work, although the other members of our party sometimes add to the supply by the skilful use of their rifles. Fishing has already been abandoned several weeks. Duck-shooting is not very remunerative, owing to the scarcity of these fowls in this region, although the photographer's skill and industry have been, and still are, occasionally rewarded by a lucky shot. The killing of the red deer has been intentionally restricted, since we came into the wilderness, to the supply of our wants, although those killed while engaged in the reconnoissance were somewhat in excess of this demand. The whole number of red deer killed by us now foot up fourteen, although we could easily have made it at least fifty. One important object of this expedition was the collection of specimens of natural history for my cabinet, and I have succeeded very satisfactorily in this direction.

During the afternoon of November 2 the captain and myself returned to Moose Hill, while George Ross and Mr. Mildenberger remained in the camp on Camp Lake. Since our recent exciting moose-hunt I am no longer satisfied with the humdrum life on Camp Lake; deer-hunting is no longer a novel and exciting pastime for me. I am this day thirsting for new fields; a grand moose- or bear-hunt; some excitement that will stimulate my heart to greater action; something that will supply mental food, will add a zest to thought and an additional motive for increased physical activity.

We reached Moose Hill about four o'clock in the afternoon and spent another night under a lean-to. The early part of the evening was passed in pleasant conversation and listening to the crackling of our hard-wood fire, which the captain says forebodes the coming of a snow-storm.

The captain's prediction was fulfilled. The ground was covered this morning with a light, tracking snow, and still the storm continued. We started, immediately after breakfast, in search of moose. The storm soon ceased; the clouds disappeared; the sun shone out brightly, which caused the snow on the trees to melt rapidly. The search for moose was a failure, but we did succeed in finding an old bear's path, which led from a small brook to the carcass of a dead moose, which we concluded had evidently died of disease, inasmuch as we were unable to find any mark of injury that had been inflicted by the sportsman. This animal had probably been dead about six weeks, and was greatly emaciated at the time of his death. We discovered, by our examination, that one knee-joint had been extensively diseased. The animal had evidently suffered with severe suppurative arthritis, which was complicated by a necrosis of all the bones entering into this joint. The antlers were imperfectly developed and still covered with velvet. This carcass was found about six miles distant from those on Moose Hill. The indications favored the opinion that the bear had been feeding on this body several weeks, since the path was well worn and much of the carcass had already been consumed.

Having now paid our respects to the path and the dead moose, we began a search for old bruin, who was soon started from a thicket near his food-supply; and here we discovered his fresh tracks in the newly-fallen snow. We now started on this trail, which was easily followed, but soon halted and held a consultation in regard to the best method of procedure. We had left Camp Lake with rations intended to supply our wants for only twenty-four hours. Should we now attempt to trail this bear to his den, or return to our camp and procure an additional supply of provisions and then establish a watch on his path? The captain reminded me of the fact that if we even succeeded in trailing the bear to his den, we were not now provided with either axe or spade with which to bring him from his cover. The force of this argument was fully appreciated, and, furthermore, it was by no means certain that old bruin would be so obliging as to conduct us direct to his residence. In many instances sportsmen have had reason to regret this hasty conclusion,—viz., that if they followed old bruin's trail he would lead them to his home; but instead of doing this he has conducted them a score of miles away from it. It is true that the conditions for trailing are unusually favorable this morning, owing to the presence of the fresh snow, which faithfully records every impression made in it. The real question is, What shall we do under these circumstances? This brings up for consideration the other side of the question. It should be remembered that the bear has been started from his cover in the thicket, and that we have been tramping about the dead moose and along bruin's path. Bruin may have sighted us, and it is very certain that he has already scented us. Therefore it may be very properly questioned whether or not he will return to his present food-supply. It is generally believed that this animal is not easily frightened away from his food, or rather, that he will return time and again after he has been driven away from it, especially when the supply is not abundant. Furthermore, this inclination to come back to his food seems to increase with every repetition which he makes for this purpose until the supply is exhausted. It then seemed entirely reasonable for us to presume in this case that our game would return to his old haunts under the promptings of hunger; inasmuch as the food-supply in this region was extremely limited at this time. We, therefore, concluded it was better to make no further effort to follow bruin, but to return at an early day and establish a watch on his pathway leading from the brook to the dead moose.

In accordance with this resolution we soon started on our return to Camp Lake, where we arrived before nightfall; found Mr. Mildenberger and George Ross seated near the camp-fire in the full enjoyment of their freedom from toil, recalling their past sports and contemplating new pleasures to be gleaned from the chase in the near future. It was the intention of the captain and myself, when we reached here to-day, to provide ourselves with food enough to last four or five days, and such other articles as might be required during our intended sojourn in the vicinity of old bruin's food-supply, and return to the spot to-morrow morning; but in this instance it was not many hours before we fully appreciated the fact that

> "The best laid schemes o' mice an' men
>    Gang aft a-gley,
>  An' lea'e us nought but grief and pain
>    For promised joy."

It was observed during the early part of the evening that the moon shone with peculiar brightness; but before ten o'clock the atmosphere became slightly hazy, and we discovered that the satellite of the earth was encircled by a luminous halo, which has long been attributed to refraction and reflection of the rays of light by the presence of minute snow-crystals in the upper strata of the air. The existence of this phenomenon, therefore, gave rise to no small degree of anxiety on my part; and the feeling of despondency was momentarily increased by the commencement of a severe snow-storm before three o'clock the next morning. This storm continued without abatement for thirty hours, and during this period there had fallen twenty inches of snow. The severity of the storm kept us confined to our camp throughout the entire day; and, consequently, the 4th of November, 1884, will long be remembered by us for other reasons than the election of a Democratic President of the United States. The question uppermost in my mind during this gloomy period was that involving the capture of the bear. The captain expressed the firm conviction that the bear would now disappear within his den, and remain there until the ides of March had made their appearance. This was very disagreeable information for the author, and he sought to controvert the opinion thus expressed by the citation of the doubts expressed on this point by Frank Forester and other authorities. It must, however, be admitted that this self-imposed task was found to be very difficult, inasmuch as these authorities generally acknowledge that old bruin usually dens up with the coming of the first heavy snow in autumn, and very rarely leaves his winter chamber until the approach of genial spring. The author will be subsequently pleased to inform the reader in regard to the behavior of this particular bear, although he may be assured that it was most unsatisfactory.

This record has been brought down to the 5th of November, which finds us nearly buried beneath the snow, while the cold wind comes to us this morning from the northwest. The snow-storm continues, but is less severe than it was yesterday, although the weather is colder. The lakes are freezing rapidly, and it is with much difficulty that we can pass our canoes through the ice that has already formed, and it is very evident that navigation in this region will be closed within a few hours.

The captain and the author took their departure from the buried tent on Camp Lake about half-past nine o'clock this morning. The sun had already made a few ineffectual attempts to send forth her cheering rays, but the rapidly-moving veil of clouds which covered its face has thus far defeated this benign effort. The wind is blowing; it causes the snow to fly in a very lively style from the evergreen-trees, on which some still reposes; while in addition to this, there are numerous attempts to renew the snow-storm. The paddling of our canoe requires the united efforts of the captain and myself, since it is necessary that one should be almost constantly breaking the ice with the paddle while the other pushes the frail bark forward. Neither was our progress on land more rapid or less laborious, since we were compelled to wallow through the deep snow, which also served to cover fallen trees, bushes, etc., while these in turn frequently entrapped our feet and plunged us headlong into this cold bed. The author is rather reluctantly compelled to admit, at this late date, that he received much more than his share of these rough tumbles, inasmuch as the captain's superior knowledge of wood-craft, as well as his greater activity, enabled him to avoid many of these undesirable somersaults, although the most disagreeable feature connected with them was the continued sensation so closely resembling that produced by a cold-water bath. The snow on these occasions insinuated itself into my ears, around my neck and wrists, in which places it soon melted, and then as water was carried to every part of my body.

The author, even at this moment, has a very distinct recollection that, during the greater part of that memorable day, his hands were so much benumbed with cold that it was found very difficult to handle either the paddle or rifle. Fortunately, however, for his present happiness, he was able even then to look forward to a more favorable state of existence, apparent in the near future, in which all these efforts would be rewarded by new sports and more favorable conditions.

We reached our lean-to on Moose Hill about one o'clock in the afternoon, which we had left standing when we visited this spot. It was now almost buried beneath the snow, while its interior was nearly filled with the same material, which had been carried there by the driving wind. When we left here on the morning of the 3d of November the captain had hung up a large piece of venison on a tree, in order that it might be beyond the reach of wolves, foxes, and other meat-eating animals; he had also placed some bread beneath the cover of our lean-to, and, therefore, it was not deemed necessary to bring with us any venison this morning when we left Camp Lake. Here we were again disappointed. During our absence the ravens had taken possession of the venison and caused it to disappear, notwithstanding the fact that there was an abundance of moose-meat in the immediate vicinity. We also relied on the bread which we had placed beneath our blankets, but only for our dinner; this was frozen, and, although we had brought flour with us, we could not tarry long enough here to bake bread. Our dinner, therefore, consisted of a cup of hot tea and some frozen cramper. We are not, however, discouraged, since we are in possession of our rifles and an abundance of ammunition. Consequently we can very soon supply meat. Having completed our frugal meal, we promptly started for our destination. The immediate objective-point was Trout Lake, which was reached in due time, and here we entered once more our canoe. The paddling of this craft was even more difficult now than it was in the morning, since the ice was constantly becoming thicker. So great was the effort to propel the canoe that it caused the captain and myself to perspire freely. This was, however, a very pleasant change from walking in the woods while the cold water was coursing down our backs. There were still a few places in the lake where ducks could succeed in finding a small open space, and in one of these open spots we discovered a flock of these fowls. At the moment we discovered them I suppose we were fully six hundred yards away. We continued to paddle forward cautiously until we had shortened the range to about three hundred yards, when I raised my rifle and forwarded my compliments. One fine bird in the flock promptly acknowledged the receipt of the same by the loss of her head and turning up her feet. This was our prompt commencement in providing flesh food for our larder, and the success of the shot gave us much satisfaction. We pulled away on our paddles, picked up our game, and then headed for that point on the shore where we intended to disembark. Breaking the ice with the paddle was now becoming perceptibly more difficult every hour, and the lapse of a very brief period will render it an impossibility. The shore was finally reached, the canoe taken from the water, and, after being turned bottom upward, was placed on some brush, while the captain remarked, " Navigation is closed; we shall have no further use for little birch-barks this year." The tramp was at this point again resumed, and we pushed forward as rapidly as was possible under the circumstances for our destination. The captain aimed to reach a little hut which he had constructed some years previously, while trapping in this part of the forest, before nightfall, in order to spend the night in it.

The storm had now ceased; the sun shone out, but it was nevertheless very cold. The game had commenced to move about, although during the storm it had remained under cover and was inactive. We saw tracks of the red deer and the moose. It was about five o'clock when we arrived at the trapper's cabin. We were once more disappointed: we had hoped for shelter and there was none. The roof of this cabin had fallen in, evidently some months previously, and consequently its interior was filled with snow, while the side walls were yet standing. There was no time to be lost. The necessary preparations must be made for the night. It was determined to remove the snow and débris from the cabin in order that we might occupy it. Both the captain and myself set to the performance of this work with much energy. It was now more pleasant to work than to remain idle. Work brought with it warmth and comfort, while inactivity was attended with a chattering of the teeth and physical suffering. These efforts did not cease until we had in some measure accomplished our object. The snow and rubbish had been partially removed and a new roof placed on the old walls of the cabin. The fire was built within this structure; a hole in the roof nearly four feet square had been left for the escape of the smoke, besides which great openings remained in the side walls and roof, through which the starry heavens were visible. The evening meal consisted of an abundance of hot cramper and tea; we had reserved the duck for our breakfast. The only blankets we had with us had been dug up from beneath the snow that had drifted under the lean-to on Moose Hill, and were, therefore, wet. We spent much of the evening in attempting to dry them before our fire. These blankets were finally arranged within the cabin and we attempted to secure sleep, but the cold was so intense as to seriously interfere with this purpose, although the physical efforts made by us during the day strongly predisposed us in this direction. The captain was up and moving two hours before the dawn of day. He promptly, after rising, paid special attention to the fire; the increased warmth diffused itself through the cabin, and thus afforded me a better opportunity to secure some refreshing sleep, which, it is hardly necessary for me to say, I willingly improved. It was not until day-break that I aroused myself and made ready for breakfast, which had already been elegantly prepared by my guide.

## CHAPTER XII.

The Bear which was not killed—Following the Moose—The Captain killed the Bull Moose—Packing out of the Woods—The Rest at Harkness's Shack—A Hard Tramp—Burk's Falls—A Deer-Hunt—Another Trip to Canada in the Company of my Son, a Lad of Fifteen—Teaching the Boy to Shoot—Killed his First Deer—An Exciting Chase—The Old Doe makes her Escape.

HE reader left us busied in our miserable cabin with our morning meal, which having been completed, we started off for the old bear's food-supply. This point was distant from the cabin something less than a mile, and was, therefore, reached within half an hour after the start was made. We found that the dead moose had not been visited by old bruin since the heavy snow-fall; although a flock of ravens had uncovered the carcass and were engaged in picking the flesh from his bones at the moment of our arrival. The prospect of meeting the game which we sought, it must be confessed, was now very discouraging; but, nevertheless, I was determined to remain on the watch here for the present. The captain cut out some of the underbrush in order that I might be better enabled to discover the approach of the much-desired visitor, and then left me, saying, "I will go off in search of other game." I remained on this lonely bear-watch about five hours, and then went to hunt the moose or deer. I followed the first trail that I struck. It had been made by a red deer; was still fresh, but soon crossed another trail which had been left by three moose. This trail had evidently been made on the previous day while it was still snowing, and the tracks had been, in some measure, obscured from

Food for the ravens left by bruin.

this cause. I plodded along slowly on this trail about one hour, when I was greatly delighted to find it crossed by another which was fresh and made by the same number of animals. I immediately turned away from the old trail and started off on the fresh one. Within twenty minutes I discovered that the new trail had been made within half an hour, and was, therefore, encouraged to push forward, hoping to strike these animals before nightfall. The deep snow seriously impeded my progress; but, nevertheless, I soon came on their warm beds, from which they had just risen, about three o'clock in the afternoon. I am not certain whether they were frightened from their repose by my incautious approach, but think it more probable that they scented me because of an unfavorable wind. However, they succeeded in getting away without receiving my fire.

Their retreat was made in good order and without any unseemly haste. I continued the pursuit an hour longer, until warned by the sinking sun that it was time to turn my face towards our hut, which was now distant from me at least eight miles. It was with a heavy heart that I retraced my steps without knowing that our larder was yet supplied with meat. I was overtaken in this great forest by the shades of night while yet four or five miles from the camp, although the stars shone out brightly in the absence of the sunlight, and the moon soon came up to light me along my way.

I halted by the side of the dead moose to ascertain if old bruin had been there for his meal, but my examination soon convinced me that he had fully determined to wait for more pleasant weather before he resumed eating. Therefore it only remained for me to hasten on to the hut, where I was fully assured that I would be heartily welcomed by the captain.

I arrived at my destination in due time. The first

object which attracted my attention was the cheerful blaze of the wood fire, after which my eyes fell on the bull moose's head lying just outside of the hut. It was now plain that the captain's hunt had been rewarded by killing a moose. After inspecting, by the moonlight and the light from the fire, this head and the antlers, I entered the hut, where I saw hanging on the wall an abundance of moose-meat. A single glance at the captain's face convinced me that he was happy. He greeted me pleasantly, and I promptly inquired of him in regard to the sport of the day. He briefly detailed his doings; informed me that he had seen several moose after he parted from me in the morning, but had killed only a single animal. He was inclined to think that he had not been as successful in killing game as was demanded by the circumstances of the case. I inquired in regard to the number of shots that he had fired during the day, and he replied, "I don't know; the number is less than thirty." He furthermore added that he had shot eighteen times at the bull which he killed before the animal ceased to show signs of life. The reader may here find himself inclined to think that the captain should be classed among amateur sportsmen, but I will only say that it would be a very difficult task to find an expert that could kill as much game in these woods as my old guide. The repeating-rifle has brought about a change in the methods of killing game. The sportsman no longer refuses to fire a shot unless he is certain that his bullet will enter some vulnerable point in the animal, but shoots away, and trusts by this means that, should he fail to kill promptly, he will at least succeed in effecting a change in the position of the game that may enable him to make a more effective shot the next time; prompted by this idea, the shooting goes on until the game has been killed or makes its escape. The captain shoots with great rapidity, and, consequently, frequently fires several shots after the mortal wound has been inflicted. In moose-, bear-, and deer-hunting he does not cease his fusillade so long as the animal shows any indications of even a lingering vitality.

The second night that we spent in this miserable hut was passed somewhat more comfortably than the first. This was owing partially to the fact that during the second night the weather moderated considerably, and our blankets were in a better condition. Furthermore, the captain had spent some time in closing the chinks between the logs after his return from the moose-hunt, and had likewise carefully prepared the wood for the fire. I take from my diary the following dull and unromantic statement of facts:

*Friday, November* 6, 1884.—The captain started from the hut this morning promptly after we had breakfasted on moose-meat, tea, and cramper, with the intention of following up the trail which I had abandoned at three o'clock on the previous day. He casually remarked when he left me that he might not be out more than three or four hours, as it seemed likely to rain. I commenced the preparation of the moose-head for transportation and mounting immediately after his departure, and was steadily engaged in the performance of this work from nine o'clock A.M. until four o'clock P.M. It was cloudy in the morning, but cleared before noon. The snow melted slightly during the day. About half-past four o'clock I started out to look after the bear; found the moose-carcass; saw a pine-marten in the act of leaving it; he climbed a tree; I shot him and then returned to camp. The bear has not visited the dead moose since the heavy snow-storm that commenced early Tuesday morning. The captain has not yet returned to camp, although it is now rapidly becoming dark. I spent an hour in procuring a supply of wood for our fire, which we are compelled to keep burning all night. I was doomed to spend the night in a miserable hut without a companion, since the captain did not return until about ten o'clock Saturday morning. He brought with him two companions to assist in transferring our luggage to Harkness's Clearings.

Prior to our start he cooked some moose-meat, and we all partook of the hastily-prepared lunch, and then promptly commenced the homeward journey. The hunt was ended, but in leaving the forest we saw many fresh moose-tracks. The game was evidently moving about in a lively fashion this morning, but we were not inclined to spend any more time in the chase.

The captain readily explained his absence from the camp on the preceding night by informing me that the trail which he had taken up soon after our separation on the previous morning was the same that I had followed so industriously the day that he had killed the bull moose near our present encampment. This trail finally brought him within a few miles of Harkness's cabin; and, inasmuch as it was then about sunset, he concluded to take lodging with his old friend and return to me the next morning.

He had found the animals which he was trailing rather shy, and consequently had only once during the day succeeded in getting within gunshot of them. A single shot fired at long range was therefore the sum total of his day's work.

His absence from my camp during the entire night had been attended with some inconvenience to myself, but with very little anxiety, since his knowledge of woodcraft and the use of firearms was a sufficient guarantee that he would turn up all right. I am free to confess, however, that the want of companionship was keenly felt during his absence.

We had previously arranged in regard to our departure from the woods, and it was therefore entirely in harmony with my wishes to find myself, on the evening of the 7th of November, once more in the company of my photographer and George Ross, the junior guide. The entire party, in accordance with the prearranged plans, have this day united at Mr. Harkness's cabin,* who supplies us with very good meals, while we are comfortably lodged in a log cabin built near his own by Mr. Wood, who has since married the daughter of our host.

Here the adventures of the last two months were again reviewed, and here, again, we joyfully recalled the sports and hardships in which we had so recently participated. We had gathered during our hunt a large number of trophies, and had likewise secured many valuable negatives. It was, therefore, with much satisfaction that we summed up the results of this expedition.

* See tail-piece Chapter XI.

Sunday, November 8, was spent quietly by our party at Harkness's place, although it was found necessary to make some preparation for our departure. The day passed slowly; seemed unusually long; probably because we were now anxious to get home, to meet again with our families. Nearly two months have elapsed since either Mr. Mildenberger or myself have received any tidings from Jersey City, but we expect to find letters awaiting our arrival at Spence. We were up and had breakfast before daylight the next morning. The ox-team had been yoked

A hard tramp—homeward bound.

and were hitched to the old jumper before the first rays of the morning light were visible in the east. The gray dawn of the morning found us moving homeward through the stiffened snow, which was now about twelve inches deep; traversing a broad swamp which had not yet been closed by the cold frosts of autumn; travelling on a trackless and miserable wood-road where the oxen wallowed deep in the mud, while the pedestrians occasionally sank so deeply into these sloughs as to require the assistance of a companion to extricate them. The old jumper fared no better. It frequently sank deeply into the mud and became entangled with the roots of trees and the adjacent rocks, thus bringing our team to a full halt, and commonly compelling them to remain in this position until levers had been procured, by the proper use of which we were always enabled to elevate and disengage our jumper and finally proceed on our journey. The old jumper after a while became so weakened by these repeated strains as to show marked indications of a rapidly-approaching dissolution. It, in fact, became necessary to strengthen our frail vehicle in all its parts before we reached the objective-point for which we started with the jumper this morning, although it was distant from Harkness's cabin only six miles.

The morning hours were thus passed, and it was nearly two o'clock in the afternoon before we reached our first stopping-place. The jumper was now a complete wreck, and the oxen were wet with their perspiration and well bespattered with mud. We had previously arranged with Mr. Cunningham to provide for us a dinner and then take our luggage forward from this point to Burk's Falls with a horse-team. The dinner was awaiting our arrival; the team was soon placed before the wagon and our luggage was transferred to it. The halt made here did not exceed forty-five minutes, when the tramp was again resumed. The circumstances now seemed more favorable to our progress. We had reached the Queen's Highway. The fall of snow had not been so deep here as in the woods, and had probably melted down rapidly; therefore there were here visible a few bare spots of earth, although the road on which we are to travel has been recently constructed and is now a perfect bed of mud. I started off in company with the captain, taking a route across the fields and through the woods. The photographer and George Ross have preceded us. Cunningham's horses drag the heavily-loaded wagon slowly along the highway. The pedestrian is able to make better time than these horses under the circumstances. A brisk walk of three miles enabled the captain and myself to overtake the photographer and the junior guide. It was during this walk, and prior to the overhauling of our companions, that we chanced to come upon a wood-chopper, who was engaged in levelling the forest preparatory to clearing it for cultivation. He had previously been informed that we had left the woods and were now homeward bound, carrying with us a wagon-load of trophies. He, therefore, began to question the captain in regard to our unsurpassed success in hunting; and while they were engaged in this conversation I espied a meat-bird sitting on the top branches of a tree about six rods distant from me. The sight of the bird prompted me to raise my rifle and fire a shot, which chanced to drop the bird to the ground. The wood-chopper quickly rushed away with the instincts of a retriever, and soon returned with the dead bird in his hand, which he promptly delivered to me. He instantly remarked, "I am not surprised that you have secured a wagon-load of trophies after seeing you drop that small bird at such a long distance." He was now evidently anxious to see me make another trial of my skill with the rifle, since he soon pointed out another bird of the same species within the range of my gun. I had made a good shot, and did not care to repeat the effort lest I might not add to my reputation as a marksman; and, consequently, I now placed my gun in the captain's hands and requested him to try his skill. He fired two shots and killed a bird each time, although they were not within a short range. The woodchopper was now apparently greatly impressed, and asked permission to examine the rifle, which he was promptly allowed to do. He seemed to admire the gun very much, and asked many questions about its cost, etc., and then complained that the backwoodsmen were so badly supplied with firearms. He finally remarked that if they possessed better guns they could then supply themselves with meat,— an article which was very seldom seen in these poor cabins.

This wayside chat was now brought to an end, and we bade our new-made acquaintance "good-by," and once more resumed our tramp. Half an hour later we came up with the photographer and the junior guide. The captain now suggested that he would wait by the roadside until the wagon carrying the trophies should come up, in order to render the driver such assistance as he might require on the rough road. I now went forward in company with the photographer and George Ross. The road was in a horrible condition; mud and water greatly impeded our progress, while in many places the clay held so tenaciously to our feet that it was very fatiguing to move forward even at a slow pace, consequently we plodded slowly along. It was five o'clock when we reached Berryville. We were then five miles from Burk's Falls. At this point we entered a small country store and learned that Mr. Cleveland had been elected President of the United States during our absence. It had now been more than six weeks since we had seen a newspaper. The photographer and myself were highly pleased with the result of this election. Crackers and cheese were obtained and sufficed to appease our hunger, but our soreness was only increased by this halt. The shades of night had gathered about us before we renewed our journey. We were, therefore, compelled, when we left the store and started off again for our objective-point, to walk in the middle of the road; it was no longer possible to pick our way or choose our path, since the darkness was so great as to render invisible every object situated more than three feet from us. At every step taken in this mud we sank into it deeply, sometimes even to our knees. It was no longer possible to walk erect and pursue a straight course, but we reeled about like drunken men, so great was our fatigue. Horrible! horrible! was this severe ordeal! We could not halt for the night. No shelter could be had after we left Berryville until we reached Burk's Falls. Our situation was no longer enjoyable. We had undertaken to perform a very difficult task, too great a labor; but the plan could not be changed, and therefore we pushed forward. We finally arrived at our hotel about eight in the evening. We were foot-sore and weary. George Ross, a strong backwoodsman, was pale and trembled in every muscle; my feet were badly blistered and greatly swollen. I could scarcely stand; removed my shoes as quickly as possible after I entered the hotel. Sent to the store and purchased a pair of arctics, which I promptly donned after taking a foot-bath. The junior guide was thoroughly exhausted and began to vomit soon after our arrival. Should the reader venture to think that our condition was in some measure dependent on the use of alcoholic stimulants, allow me to inform him that no man in our party has tasted a drop of strong drink during the last six weeks. Nothing has been said in regard to the condition of our photographer at the time of our arrival. I think it must be admitted that he had passed through this trying ordeal somewhat more fortunately than either George Ross or myself, but he frankly admitted that he had never been so greatly fatigued prior to this tramp. We had walked to-day twenty miles, but could have made fifty with more ease had the condition of the roads been favorable to such an effort. I retired to my room, which was well warmed, at an early hour; but notwithstanding the precaution taken I was seized with a chill, which lasted about half an hour. The wagon with our trophies did not arrive until eleven o'clock that night. Darkness and the bad condition of the roads had been the cause of the delay. The team was a very strong one and in a very good condition for heavy work.

Having passed the night tolerably well, our party met at the breakfast-table the following morning about nine o'clock somewhat refreshed. A party of deer-hunters living in this village had proposed a deer-hunt to the captain and wished us to join them in this sport. The hunt was to take place near the village, and we were informed that the run-ways could be reached by a buck-board wagon. It was impossible for us to leave here until the following morning, since "Ponto" had wearied during the long tramp of the previous day and found a new home at Berryville. It had already been settled that George Ross should procure a horse and saddle and return for the purpose of bringing up the straggler. Therefore, after considerable consideration of this subject, I rather reluctantly consented to become one of the hunting-party. A buck-board wagon was procured for the use of a circuit judge—who was one of the party—and myself, and we were duly driven to a run-way which it had been decided that we were to watch.

The occurrences of the morning were very similar to those which have been already so frequently described. The music made by the hounds was very exciting, and the deer was killed by the captain. We returned to the village after the single race and spent the balance of the day in the hotel.

Thus ended the grandest hunt in which it has ever been my good fortune to participate. It is true that we endured many hardships, but we were more than amply compensated for all these by the pleasures of the chase. We returned to our professional duties reinvigorated and better prepared for the discharge of those efforts demanded of us, both mental and physical.

The question may be raised by the reader if it were not possible to have avoided many of the severe tramps and likewise some of the exposure. This inquiry must be answered in the affirmative, since it must be self-evident to every reader that the amount of tramping done in any particular case will depend largely on the inclination of the sportsman. In deer-hunting it is quite possible to avoid any degree of exercise which will be fatiguing, especially when hounds are employed. The sportsman may have his tent erected near the point where the hunt is to take place, and thus avoid the necessity of any tramping. He can proceed in his canoe to any point of the lake which it is deemed advisable to watch, or should he elect to watch a run-way, the location of his tent may be such that the walk would not be fatiguing. Lake-hunting is commonly practised in this region, and there are probably ninety-nine deer killed in the water where there is one killed on the run-ways when hounds are employed.

In still-hunting the sportsman may determine for himself the amount of walking which he will do; but the results of the hunt will depend very largely upon the energy and industry of the sportsman, especially if the other factors of success are equal. The red deer are very abundant throughout this entire region, and may be successfully hunted in close proximity to the settlers' cabins. The same is true of the ruffed grouse. There is likewise very excellent bass- and pickerel-fishing in nearly all the lakes and rivers in the sparsely-settled districts, but those who desire really good trout-fishing, except during the early part of the month of June, must go back into the forests. A single day's journey from a railroad depot will, however, suffice to bring the fisherman into a region where his efforts, even in autumn, will be rewarded by the capture of the speckled beauties. This region of country in which I have hunted may be very readily reached by the Northern Railroad from Toronto, Canada; while the sportsman may very well procure the necessary supply of provisions from any of the small villages on this line. Supplies may be had of excellent quality and in any desired quantity at Burk's Falls. Hotel accommodation is, likewise, abundant and of such a character as to satisfy most sportsmen. I think it is highly probable that some sportsmen may prefer to remain in a hotel and do their shooting in the immediate neighborhood of the same, although much better results may be obtained by tenting on the field selected for the sport. The author likewise believes that the sportsman will add greatly to his enjoyment by the latter course of procedure, which certainly possesses for most men a charm independent of the increased facilities it affords for procuring game.

I recently spent a few days very pleasantly in the vicinity of Maganetawan in deer-hunting and partridge-shooting, in company with my son, a youth of fifteen years, and inasmuch as it illustrates the possibility of obtaining very good sport without any great fatigue or exertion, I am disposed to give a brief description of this trip, which I think may not be devoid of interest. We started from our home in Jersey City, New Jersey, August 31, 1886. An evening train on the New York, Lake Erie and Western Railroad carried us forwards towards our destination. The next morning found us at Niagara Falls, where we spent the most of the day in sight-seeing, but we reached Toronto at a late hour of the same evening. The following morning we were moving forward by the Northern Railroad towards Muskoka. In due time we arrived at the village of Maganetawan, where we were very cordially received by the fat and genial proprietor of a hotel which bears the same name as the village in which it is located. He had been informed, prior to our arrival, by the captain that we were *en route* for the woods, and might be expected in this village at the date on which we reached it, and consequently we were not unexpected guests. In accordance with a previous arrangement made with Captain Ross, he put in an appearance at our hotel the next morning at an early hour. He had brought with him a wagon to transport us and our baggage to the lake of "Many Islands," where it had already been determined the hunt should take place.

We reached our destination Saturday, September 5, at about half-past three o'clock. This lake is situated about eleven miles from the village of Maganetawan, and our baggage was delivered by the wagon within half a mile of its shore. Inasmuch as the latter portion of the road we had traversed had been found to be rather rough, we had therefore chosen to walk about three miles. The scene presented by this lake on our arrival was highly pleasing. There lay spread out before us a magnificent sheet of pure water stirred by a slight breeze, which produced little ripples on its surface, that sparkled with the brilliance of diamonds surrounded with bright silver in the clear sunlight of a cloudless autumn day. The lake of "Many Islands" is very similar to many others in this "Lake Land of Canada." It is about three miles in length and one mile in width, while its numerous islands prevent us from seeing but a small portion of it from any point which may be selected on its shore.

At the time of our visit it was completely surrounded

by a virgin forest of hard wood, interspersed with giant pines; but it was then expected that the lumbermen would soon commence their work of devastation, which will not end until the whole neighborhood has been robbed of the pine timber.

The sun was shining brightly when we reached the shore of this lake, and the weather was oppressively warm. We, therefore, reclined on the moss which grew in great abundance, even quite near the water's edge, until sufficiently rested to begin the labor required to erect our tent and perform such other duties about the camp as seemed to be necessary for our comfort. Myself and son are accompanied by the captain and two other guides, consequently the preparation of the camp is quickly effected. We are now ready to start out for some fishing. My son and myself were soon seated in a large, birch-bark canoe, and the captain was working the paddle. We have each thrown a trolling-line into the water, and the bass have promptly responded to our glittering invitations. We had soon captured a fine lot of these delicious fish, and among them there was one large one, supposed to weigh fully four pounds.

We returned to our camp in time to have some fish prepared for our evening meal. The sun disappeared below the western horizon soon after we had finished our supper, and the evening breeze seemed to possess just those qualities best adapted to make life agreeable; was neither too warm nor too cool. This was my son's first night passed under canvas, and he was perfectly charmed with the new condition of things. He slept soundly and arose early the following morning greatly refreshed, while mental visions of delight rapidly chased each other through his brain. He was now very anxious and almost impatient to engage in a deer-hunt. It was, therefore, with marked joy that he heard the captain declare that he would send the hounds into the woods immediately after breakfast. The morning was warm,—almost sultry,—and the trees were covered with a heavy green foliage, but as soon as the breakfast had been eaten the captain directed "Tom," one of the guides, to start with the hounds into the woods and send us a deer. "Tom" obeyed this order with alacrity, while the captain and "Jim" cleared away the remnants of the morning repast and put in order the "camp-kit."

They spent about twenty minutes in this labor, and the captain then announced his readiness for us to enter the canoes. Both Henry and myself entered his canoe, which he immediately shoved into the lake, and then paddled us off about one mile to an island situated near the head of this body of water. "Jim" had followed us in a canoe. Both canoes were drawn upon this island and we promptly stepped on the dry land. The captain now carefully surveyed the surroundings for the purpose of selecting the most advantageous places for the watch. Having satisfied himself in regard to this matter, he then said to me, "Doctor, you will go with me in my canoe and your son will watch with 'Jim.'"

I looked at Henry and instantly discovered that he was disappointed. I had previously informed him that the captain was the most competent guide, and that I should therefore leave him in his charge, in order that he might have an opportunity to kill the game. The reader will now readily comprehend the cause of the lad's disappointment. I now informed the captain of my desire in this matter, and he promptly consented to this arrangement, which placed Henry in his charge. The boy's face instantly lighted up and he was again happy. The captain now gave "Jim" the necessary instructions, and we started for the point which had been designated for our watch. The sun was shining brightly, and there was only a slight breeze at this time on the lake.

Having reached our destination, the canoe was now drawn on the land, and I seated myself beneath the shade of a friendly bush, while "Jim" remained standing in order to have a better view of the surroundings. About half an hour was thus spent, when I was suddenly startled by a heavy splash in the water and an exclamation from my guide, who, in a loud whisper, announced the presence of a buck in the water. I promptly arose to my feet and discovered, with the guide's assistance, our game swimming out towards the centre of the lake. This charming vision was only momentary, since the animal promptly disappeared behind one of the many islands that grace the lake. Our canoe was quickly pushed into the lake and quietly entered. We then pulled away with all our might, although we were now confident that the captain had already discovered the prize and was moving for its capture. A few moments later, having then rounded the island, which momentarily hid from our vision the object we sought, we again saw the deer, which was now closely pursued by the captain's canoe, while my son was seated in its bow with his gun already raised in readiness for the shot. The captain was giving him the necessary instruction. "Jim" was paddling with all his might, but we were now about five hundred yards behind the captain, while he was within thirty yards of the buck. The command was given by the captain in the following language: "Take aim at the back of the head,—fire!" A little puff of blue smoke was seen to shoot forth from the muzzle of the lad's gun; the animal's heavy antlers disappeared beneath the waters of the lake; the boy had killed his first deer and was as happy as a general who had just won his first battle. This buck's head was carefully prepared for mounting in our camp, and is now one of the boy's trophies, which he has preserved at his home and proudly exhibits to his youthful companions.

We remained encamped on this beautiful sheet of water about ten days, and during this period killed eight deer, many ruffed grouse, and caught as many fish as we desired for our table. The tent was, soon after our arrival, removed from the lake-shore—where it was at first erected—to one of the many islands in this body of water, where it remained until the day of our departure. The boy was made, in accordance with the desire which the author had expressed soon after our arrival, the hero of the hunt; and during our brief stay killed four deer and more than one-half the whole number of partridges. The hunt was practically the boy's own sport, and afforded him the highest pleasure consistent with our surroundings. It is no part of my intention, at the present time, to inflict on the reader a full report of the daily occurrences during our stay in this region, but I shall describe some of the more exciting events which transpired; and in addition to this, also detail some of the more interesting movements of the game which we were hunting.

Having sent the hounds into the woods one cloudy morning in company with "Jim," who on this day acted as our starter, I left the camp on the island in the company of the faithful "Tom," who paddled the birch-bark for me, while my son was, as usual, in the canoe with the captain. We expected the deer this morning would take to the water about one mile from our camp, and consequently the canoes were directed towards this point. I had thrown a troll into the water soon after leaving camp, in order to take some fish before the deer should put in an appearance. We listened attentively for the music of the hounds, but not a single note had been heard, when a slight crackling sound, made in the woods near the shore of the lake, attracted my attention. "Tom" had, a moment previously, raised his paddle from the water, and I had already commenced to reel in the long line in order that I might be better prepared for the arrival of the expected game.

The sounds which I have previously mentioned had not been heard by "Tom," and, in fact, were so indistinctly perceptible to my ear as to call forth no comment from me, although my eye was instinctively fixed on that portion of the shore nearest to the point where they had seemed to originate. Scarcely had one minute elapsed since I had heard the crackling sounds in the woods before a large doe made her appearance on the shore at the point which I was then watching. She did not break cover at a single bound, as is sometimes the case with the members of her family, but trotted slowly into the water, and showed, at this moment, no indications of fear or even anxiety. She had entered the lake directly in front of our canoe, although possibly about six hundred yards distant from us. The course at first taken in the water was directly towards us, and we were very careful to make no movement which might attract her attention. She swam out into the lake about eighty yards, apparently entirely uninfluenced by any sense of fear or danger; but now began to sniff the air, move her ears and then turn her head in various directions, evidently endeavoring to sight the object which she had already scented. During this period she made very slow progress in swimming, although still coming towards us, but at a very slow rate of speed; and finally, when about one hundred yards from the shore, she turned up the lake and continued to swim at about the same distance from the land. She had now headed directly towards the captain's canoe, which was probably two thousand yards distant from her. She still continued to turn her head occasionally towards our canoe,—evidently expecting that an enemy would assail her from that direction. Her nervous movements were still expressive of anxiety. We had hoped that she would leave the shore, and thus afford us an opportunity to bring our canoe between her and the land; but her movements were entirely unfavorable for the accomplishment of this object.

The captain had carefully watched her from the moment

when he had first discovered her in the lake, which was only a few moments after she broke cover. He, too, remained inactive for a while, for the same reasons that had prompted us to this course, particularly because the animal was so near to the shore that she could easily put herself, with little loss of time, on dry land. He finally tired of this inactivity and started energetically forward in the chase. Both "Tom" and myself had been carefully watching him, and consequently recognized the first stroke which he made with his paddle. The scene was now very interesting and highly picturesque; the old doe was likely to be surprised; she was still looking for an enemy to appear from the lower part of the lake, having already scented us, while the captain was coming down on her from the head of the same waters. Behold the enemy! There they come. The boy sits motionless in the bow of the canoe; his right hand rests gently on the breech of his gun; the captain is near the stern of the frail bark; his strong arms work vigorously and noiselessly the paddle. The little vessel moves rapidly forward in a straight line, but its movements are noiseless although the water fairly boils about its bow and stern. They are now within five hundred yards of the prize; the deer is still swimming towards them; at this moment "Tom" placed his paddle in the water and entered the race. A few minutes later she discovered the captain's canoe bearing down upon her, and promptly turned around in the water and commenced a desperate effort to reach the run-way by which she entered the lake. Behold her frantic efforts! She is maddened by the appearance of an unexpected enemy; she struggles desperately in the water; raises herself high into the air and then settles down to her grandest efforts in swimming. Both canoes are rapidly closing in upon her; she has discovered the danger of her situation. The captain's canoe is now within a hundred yards of the frightened deer; but "Tom" is still more than four hundred yards away. The boy has raised his gun; is taking aim. Puff goes the smoke from the muzzle of his fowling-piece; the charge of buckshot passed a little above her head and she is unharmed. The boy is now making a desperate effort to remove the empty shell from his single-barrel breech-loading gun. The captain has brought the canoe within sixty yards of the old doe. Behold them! He has dropped the paddle, taken the gun from the boy's hand, and is now endeavoring to remove the empty shell, which he accomplished after the loss of a few seconds of valuable time. The gun is then handed back to the boy, after having been reloaded, but the distance between the floating canoe and the rapidly-swimming deer has increased during this interval. "Tom," on the contrary, has succeeded in bringing his canoe within about two hundred yards of the game; but the deer is now almost ready to leap on the shore. I have seized my repeating Winchester rifle and will try a shot at the escaping animal. Two shots are fired in rapid succession: one before she had raised from the water and the other just as she leaped on the dry land, but she has not halted at my command. The captain failed to bring the deer within the range of the boy's gun after it was reloaded. Thus ended a very exciting chase.

## CHAPTER XIII.

The Continuance of the Deer-Hunt—An Exciting Chase—Brilliant Manœuvring of an Old Buck—Breaking Camp on the Island—A Partridge-Hunt by the Roadside—An Exciting Race between "Jim" and the Old Cocker Spaniel—Our Return to Maganetawan—The Trip from Maganetawan to Toronto.

THE details of the morning hunt have already been given, but there still remains to be described a more exciting chase, which occurred in the afternoon of the same day. The morning of this day was cloudy, but the evening was cool and cloudless, while the sun shone out brightly.

It was therefore determined soon after the mid-day meal that "Jim" should go again into the woods with the hounds and try to send us a deer. In accordance with this determination he was promptly moving away from our camp with the hounds in the canoe.

The other canoes followed him after a delay of about half an hour. The captain was again in the company of my son, while I was attended by "Tom," as in the morning. We expected the deer would come to the lake by the same run-way as was chosen by the old doe in the morning. The captain, however, stationed "Tom's" canoe about one mile from the point where the doe entered the water. He, however, selected an advantageous position for himself and the lad, which was much nearer to this point. The afternoon dragged slowly away without the occurrence of any exciting event until after four o'clock. The waters of the lake were motionless; scarcely moved by a single ripple. The watch for the appearance of the deer was constant and faithful, and not limited to the particular point at which he was expected to make his appearance. We were somewhat discouraged by the non-arrival of the expected visitor, when we discovered that the captain had sighted game and was already in motion. Our canoe was quickly brought into motion and headed in the direction indicated by the captain's movements, although he is more than half a mile away from us. We are thoroughly satisfied that the deer is visible to him, since he never paddles with so much energy and skill except when actually engaged in the chase. We are rapidly approaching each other, and now catch our first glimpse of the deer's head, which, in the distance, appeared not larger than a small duck resting on the surface of the water. The captain is much nearer to the game than we are at this moment. "Tom" is working the paddle as though his life depended on his individual exertion. The captain's canoe shoots through the water like a thing of life. It is a grand sight, worthy the brush of an artist. Onward, still onward, over the silvery waters of the lake rushed our canoes towards the living goal which was yet unconscious of the danger. It was a long and hard pull for those who held the paddles, but we gained rapidly on the leisurely-swimming deer. The captain had succeeded in bringing his canoe within a few hundred yards of the animal before he was discovered, but unfortunately she was at this moment only a short distance from the shore. Instantly her head was turned towards the land, and here followed the desperate efforts to make her escape, but it is an old story and I shall not now repeat it. The captain redoubled his efforts with the paddle, and "Tom" followed his example. The deer having reached a spot where she was not more than forty yards from the dry land, the captain quickly dropped the paddle and seized a Winchester repeating-rifle, which was lying in the bottom of his canoe, and began a lively fusillade, which was directed at the poor animal's head, although he was at this moment about three hundred yards from the object which he sought to pierce with the leaden bullet. "Tom" now brought our canoe within a range of about five hundred yards, when I raised my rifle and joined in the music. "Tom" continued to push forward his little bark without the slightest interruption, while the captain was floating slowly forward. Bang! bang! bang! go the rifles; the balls are skipping over the water in close proximity to the exposed head, while the animal is making the most frantic efforts to escape. She is now almost ready to leap from the water, but the captain is waiting for the favorable moment to send a bullet into her body. She has risen, when the crack of the captain's rifle is heard, and she falls back into the water again. Is she dead? No. In another instant she is again on her feet, and after taking three bounds she is covered by the friendly darkness of the forest. We now pushed forward to the spot where she had left the lake. Here we beheld her blood mingling with the water, and this confirmed the opinion which we had previously formed, that she had been wounded. "Jim" was now seen to be approaching us with the hounds in his canoe. We beckoned to him to hurry forward with the dogs. He could not hear us and did not understand our signals. "Tom" pointed his canoe towards that in which "Jim" was seated and then paddled away with all his might. "Jim" now began to comprehend what was wanted at this moment. He therefore redoubled the speed of his vessel. We were soon enabled by loud shouting to make him understand that we had wounded the deer and desired to put the hounds on her trail. He was deeply interested, and promptly entered heartily into the work. The hounds were brought to the spot where the deer left the water. They bounded excitedly from the canoe and entered the forest with ringing voices. I had *never*, previously, heard so much noise made in the same limited time by two dogs. I remarked to the captain, "Your dogs are not merely giving tongue, but they are fairly yelling;" and he replied, "They are almost maddened by the smell of blood." Their entrance into the forest was followed within a few minutes by a loud crackling in the brush, which convinced us that they were already close upon the wounded animal. A few seconds later the poor deer rushed frantically from the woods and leaped into the lake, but she still apparently remembered that on the water there was yet a merciless enemy, since she contented herself by swimming a narrow bay and then again disappeared in the dark woods.

She had thus cunningly attempted to throw the hounds off her scent, while at the same time she most adroitly avoided a contact with us. Darkness was already gathering about us, but the end had not yet been reached. The passage of the deer across this bay had been observed by our party, but we were too far away to offer any protest to this procedure. A few seconds later the hounds made their appearance on the shore where she had entered the bay. One immediately entered the water and swam across, apparently in the wake left behind the poor fugitive, while the other ran the shore. During this last performance the hounds gave no music, and their silence was almost painful to us; but the moment they started off on the trail which she had made when she left the bay, they *again yelled* with all their might.

The captain at this moment promptly turned the bow of his canoe towards the head of the lake, saying, "She must take to the water again; she cannot live in the woods." The other canoes followed slowly, while we listened attentively to the sounds uttered by the hounds. Thus we were convinced that the poor deer was painfully conscious of her own weakness, and therefore kept close to the lake that she might in an emergency leap into the water and thus escape from the hounds. The objective-point for which the captain had started was situated more than a mile from the bay which the wounded deer had crossed. The hounds followed her closely to this portion of the lake, and then their voices were suddenly silenced. The question was then quickly asked by one of our party, "What has happened?" and the response was immediately given by both the other members, "The deer has taken to the water and is again swimming."

We then listened attentively for another report in this

"We found them standing on the dry ground, while the doe was lying at their feet and the hounds were fawning about them."

case, which came to us after the lapse of about fifteen minutes. It was made by the firing of two shots from the fowling-piece. "Jim" now quickly remarked, "The boy has now taken a hand in this sport; the deer is dead, and that report was not made by the rifle." We pulled away for the upper part of the lake, which was reached in due time, and here we found the captain, who had verified the correctness of his prediction. The deer had been compelled by the hounds to take to the water again, and was killed by the boy while swimming. The same thing had happened here as in the lower portion of the lake. One of the hounds had followed her into the water, while the other remained behind on the shore. The first shot fired by the lad missed her head in the partial darkness of the evening, but the second had killed her. Before we reached the captain and the boy they had towed her ashore, and we found them standing on the dry ground, while the doe was lying at their feet and the hounds were fawning about them.

We discovered at this time that the animal had been struck by the rifle-ball in the right thigh, making a compound fracture of the femur, consequently she had been compelled to make the last run on three legs. The whole number of shots fired at her were probably about twenty. The chase was one of the most exciting that I have ever participated in, but it should not be forgotten that in the first encounter all the shots were fired from a long range.

Daylight having disappeared, we were consequently prompted to return to our camp. The deer was, therefore, placed in one of our canoes, and the hounds invited to share with us a place in our little barks, and we were off to our tents.

The reader's attention has been directed to the wonderful manifestation of intelligence or instinct on the part of this doe, which had just been killed, when she, in the one instance, took to the water in order to throw the hounds off her trail, and then very promptly returned to the woods

The dead doe.

for the purpose of avoiding a second encounter with an enemy more dreadful than the dogs. Later on we find her keeping close to the lake-shore, in order that she might be thus enabled to baffle the hounds once more if the necessity should arise.

A few days after the occurrences that we have just recorded an opportunity was again given us to study some very fine manœuvring on the part of an old buck, in order to throw the keen-scented hounds off his trail. This game was so well played that it cannot fail to interest those who read it. The hounds had been taken into the woods on this occasion by the faithful "Tom," and nearly two hours had elapsed before we heard their baying, which was as yet rather indistinct.

Knowing full well that the game was now in motion, "Jim" promptly passed from the shore on which he was standing to his canoe, which was at this moment resting lightly on the water near him. The example of my guide was quickly followed by me, and the little bark was promptly brought out into the lake, which gave us a broader view of our surroundings. The baying of the hounds was occasionally lost to us, but after the lapse of a longer or shorter interval these sounds were again audible. It was very evident to our minds that the deer, when first started by the hounds, had not moved off in a direct line for the water, but had circled about in the woods; therefore "Jim" concluded, thus early in the chase, that our hounds were running a strong buck.

The opinion here expressed is based on observation, and is supposed to have its origin in the greater strength and superior confidence possessed by these males, since the females and fawns, when started by hounds, run immediately to the water; in which, by swimming, they can easily distance their tormentors,—where, as a matter of fact, they rarely attempt to follow them.

Having gained a position on the lake which enabled us to examine the various objects along the shore for a considerable distance, we soon discovered a large buck, which was walking in the water at this time, and occasionally stopping to listen to the hounds. These animals were now rapidly approaching the lake, and every moment rendered their voices more distinct to us. The old buck did not seem to be particularly anxious for his own safety, but was, nevertheless, moving very cautiously in order to throw the hounds off his trail. He remained in the water continuously, either walking, trotting, or swimming, except when brought in contact with a point of land extending out into the lake a considerable distance, when he would boldly leave the water, cross the point, and again resume his peregrinations along the shore. In this manner the shrewd animal traversed more than a mile along the lake-shore, while we were following in our canoe behind him. He finally passed from the range of our vision for a brief period, and when next discovered by us had taken to the deep waters of the lake, and was at this moment swimming directly towards us, with the apparent intention of returning to his forest home by the same run-way by which he had left it. The hounds, in the mean while, had reached the lake, and were now following slowly along the shore. They had already ceased to give tongue and were apparently discouraged and despondent.

I had never previously witnessed, on the part of a deer, so much coolness and intelligent manœuvring as had taken place in this case. Every movement by this animal had been characterized by caution and intelligence. He was evidently on the alert, as was shown by the various attitudes which he assumed and the movements which he made. It seemed to us that he had a fixed plan which he was endeavoring to execute; and the plan itself spoke well for his intelligence; but our presence on the lake, where we had not yet been observed by him, was the sole cause of its failure and his misfortune. Having discovered him well out in the lake and swimming directly towards us, we immediately placed our canoe partially behind an island, near which it was lying at the moment of the discovery, assuming such a position that we could continue to watch the approaching animal, while we were, at the same time, unobserved. Onward he came, while his large antlers were visible in the bright sunlight, as well as his head and his large, shapely neck. Patiently we waited for the arrival of the moment when we should start boldly in the chase for him, when he should have passed so far from the land that we could be assured of overtaking him before he could reach the cover of the woods. The proper moment having arrived the canoe darted rapidly from its cover, driven forward by two paddles, while the water fairly boiled about its bow. The author was now aiding the guide in hastening forward the little bark.

The old buck had not yet discovered us, and was, therefore, swimming directly forward, as if he even desired the meeting; but be assured, my reader, that the moment he either sights or scents us he will make a change in his course and greatly accelerate his speed. On, onward we sped! On, onward he came! Two thousand yards now separated us, but we were discovered! He had dropped his ears, turned his head, and was now bounding through the water towards the nearest land, but, alas, it was too late! The victory was ours! The poor animal had been fairly ambushed! The question uppermost in my mind at this moment is, Do animals reason? In the case of this deer it seems impossible to reconcile his varied movements consistently with the belief that instinct instead of a reasoning faculty controlled his action. It was observed that he listened attentively to the baying of the hounds, and that his course and movements appeared to be based on the information thus conveyed to him. Another observation was made during this hunt bearing on the acuteness of the sense of smell in the red deer, which is regarded as worthy of a brief report in this little work. The hounds had been taken into the woods for the purpose of driving deer into the lake, while "Jim" and myself were keeping a watch on one of the many islands of this beautiful sheet of water. This island was situated about three hundred yards from the mainland, where it was thought the deer might enter. We had continued to watch about three hours, when I discovered a buck walk leisurely out of the woods and unconcernedly pass down a sloping rock to the water, which he entered unhesitatingly and without causing any noise that was perceptible at our stand. We had not heard the hounds at any time during the morning prior to the appearance of this deer, and their cry was not audible to us even at this moment. The deer, immediately after entering the water, began to swim directly towards us. We were at this moment seated in our birch-bark canoe, and remained completely immovable and cautiously observed the approaching animal. He had not placed more than eighty yards between himself and the point at which he had entered the lake when he began to exhibit signs of alarm by moving his ears, snuffing in air, and turning his head in different directions, evidently for the purpose of sighting the object which he had already discovered by the sense of smell. In this effort he was certainly unsuccessful, since he did not immediately turn towards the mainland, but began to swim away from us in a line parallel with the shore of the island on which we still remained unseen by him. The course taken by this animal was that which, with the prevailing wind, would carry him most promptly beyond the limits of the scent which unquestionably pertained to us, although it was not such as to give him the highest degree of security under the circumstances. I am thoroughly convinced that his action at this time was entirely controlled by the sense of smell, and it is, likewise, an additional argument in favor of the possession of rational faculties.

The deer-hunt on the Lake of Many Islands having been completed, it now remained for us to commence the homeward journey. An arrangement had already been made with the owner of the team that had brought us into the woods to return to the place and take out our baggage on the following day. My son was not yet satisfied with the opportunity which had been given him to shoot ruffed grouse, and therefore it was settled that the lad should have an extra day for this sport.

We were now about fifteen miles from Maganetawan village, and a little more than four miles from the Nipissing and Maganetawan road. It was therefore decided that "Jim," in company with myself and son, should leave our camp on the island the day before the team was expected to make its arrival. In accordance with this determination we took our departure about three o'clock in the afternoon. "Tom" followed with a pack, consisting of our tent, blankets, and provisions, about an hour later. We were accompanied by a cocker-spaniel and a small mongrel dog which had been previously borrowed from a settler in this region, for the purpose of aiding in our search for grouse. The morning had been rainy, and consequently the trees, which were yet covered with a heavy foliage, were still loaded with water, and, as if to add to this unfavorable condition, there were several light showers during the afternoon before we reached our destination, which was the Nipissing and Maganetawan road. Owing to the unfavorable condition of the forest there was no effort made by us to procure game during the afternoon.

This tramp was a rather dull affair, owing to the circumstances surrounding us, but the road was reached in due time. "Tom" came up with the pack soon after our arrival, and our attention was immediately given to the erection of the tent and other preparations for the night. Scarcely had these preparations been completed when a heavy rain set in, which continued until daylight the following morning. "Jim" prepared the breakfast, and we were ready to start on our tramp about seven o'clock in the morning. The woods were very wet, and consequently we had no intention of leaving the road unless seduced into such action by the barking of the dogs, which informed us of the close proximity to us of the ruffed grouse. Having completed our arrangements we were off, leaving the tent standing where it was erected the previous evening, on the roadside, while the baggage had been carefully stowed away under it. It had been previously arranged with the captain that he should superintend the gathering up of the luggage and its transportation to Maganetawan.

The morning of this start had been cloudy and threatened rain at the moment of our departure, and consequently we strapped up our waterproofs and carried them with us. We had not tramped more than a half-mile when the earnest barking of the dogs a few rods from the road proclaimed to us that they had found a partridge. "Jim" was eager for sport, and therefore disregarded the prospect of receiving a shower-bath; rushed rapidly from the road to the woods, where we soon heard him shouting to the lad to "come and kill the bird." The boy was off in the twinkling of an eye, perfectly willing to take a cold shower-bath if he could kill a single partridge.

I was surprised that "Jim" should have shown so much anxiety in regard to the lad's shooting in this particular case; but I subsequently learned that he was unable to work his gun, owing to the fact that his cartridges had been thoroughly saturated with water. The boy's arrival on the ground was a little too late, since the bird had shifted its position and they were unable to find it afterwards, although they spent fully twenty minutes in the search, and finally returned from the swamp as wet as drowned rats.

"Jim's" manner indicated that he was much chagrined by the failure, but by philosophically reasoning he had succeeded in convincing himself of the wisdom of his action, and boldly asserted that "I shall no longer dread to enter the swamp, since I care nothing for either mud or water." We now journeyed on, and were very soon informed by our dogs that they had found another partridge in the swamp, not more than ten rods from the road on which we were tramping. "Jim" instantly sprung into the woods and was quickly lost to sight; although within five minutes he reported progress by firing his shot-gun, and instantly shouted, "I have him this time!" while a few minutes later he returned to the road holding up for our inspection a large cock bird which he had killed at the first shot, while the bird was quietly settling on the branch of a small evergreen-tree.

The clouds have begun to disappear, the bright rays of sunshine are now lighting up our pathway, while the gentle zephyrs are moving the foliage of the forest-trees. The prospects of a fine day's sport are brightening at this moment. "Jim" exclaims, "We will have a good day of it yet!" while at the same time a partridge rises at the roadside,—an event which is announced to us by the barking of the cocker-spaniel. This dog had taken his position at the foot of a small tree, the branches of which even overhung the road-way, and here continued to bark lustily, thus keeping the attention of the bird until the lad sent up his compliments, which she promptly acknowledged by tumbling to the ground.

The killing of this bird gave rise to a highly ludicrous scene, which I fully appreciated at the time, and which I can never readily forget. "Jim" had previously told me that the old cocker-spaniel had a very bad habit, and would "mouth" the birds whenever he could get hold of them, while he entirely disregarded the order to "bring dead bird." The owner of this dog had, likewise, informed me that the animal had never received any training, but naturally hunted very well and was a good "treer." The instant the lad fired at this bird "Jim" sprang into the woods with the alacrity of a hound, in order to grab the falling partridge before the old cocker could get hold of him. The old cocker, however, succeeded in getting the best of "Jim," grabbed the bird in his mouth and started off at full speed, while the guide followed him on the jump, as a fox-hound might follow a hare, shouting with every bound, "*Stop! stop! drop it! drop it!*" until the woods became fairly resonant with these sounds. A few seconds later the dog emerged from the woods, still clinging to the bird, closely followed by the irate guide, who still yelled as though his life depended on this effort. Here the old dog made the fatal mistake which finally cost him the prize which he had attempted to steal. He started down the road as rapidly as he could run, but "Jim" steadily gained on him. Jim was wearing on this occasion a pair of heavy leather brogans, which contained in the soles about fifty steel spikes. These shoes, in fact, were procured by him while he was engaged in that occupation commonly designated as "*river-driving*," and these spikes were intended to nail him firmly to the floating logs, and thus prevent accident or injury from slipping. The road on which this race between the old cocker and our guide took place was nearly a mass of rocks; generally flat on the upper surface, which formed the road-bed, although they possessed many irregularities of surface, size, etc. The moment the guide and dog emerged from the woods and started off on this road they were in full view of both my son and myself. The sparks eliminated by the contact of the spikes in "Jim's" brogans with the rocks in his pathway lighted up his trail and added greatly to the ludicrousness of the scene. The race may be fairly said to have been nip and tuck, but the guide is slowly gaining on the cocker. They had run about ten rods when "Jim's" brogans were in close proximity to the old dog's tail. It seemed highly probable at this moment that the guide's spiked shoes would be used as a petard for the destruction of the fugitive thief, but no, he has determined to capture him alive! Behold them at this moment! "Jim" has dropped with the intention of seizing the old rascal with his hands. The old dog—as if anticipating this movement—has suddenly jumped to one side, and instantly turned to retrace his steps. "Jim" struck the ground with a heavy thud, but was neither killed nor severely injured by this manœuvre. The dog, however, in the mean time, has been rapidly gaining on the guide and was well started on the homeward stretch. He occasionally turned his head in order to catch a glimpse of his pursuer, but he did not halt nor even slacken his pace. "Jim" was soon on his feet again, but not until the dog had secured a good start. The guide was maddened by failure, and resumed the race with a fierce determination to win. Every second shortened the distance between the contestants when "Jim" had fairly succeeded in getting under way. The old dog seemed to fully comprehend the gravity of the situation, and occasionally turned his head for the purpose of discovering and estimating his danger. He had passed safely one-half of the home-stretch, but was at this moment compelled to drop the bird from his mouth. "Jim" was at this moment close upon the dog's heels, but he heeded not the dead bird, and was evidently determined to punish the thief. The old cocker showed at this time unmistakable signs of exhaustion and fear, and was unquestionably repentant. "Jim's" brogans were once more at the dog's caudal extremity, when he suddenly dodged aside and endeavored to reach the cover of the woods; but he was too completely exhausted to accomplish this object. He dropped to the ground and looked imploringly into "Jim's" eyes for mercy; but "Jim" heeded not the imploring looks and cringing attitude of the old rascal. He had him by the nape of the neck, and promptly administered the well-merited punishment. The old dog fairly yelled with pain, and "Jim" yelled back to him, "*Steal the boy's bird, will you? I will teach you honesty. I will, you old rascal!*"

The whole scene had been watched by the boy and myself. The comical part played by the actors can be more easily imagined than described. It caused peal after peal of laughter from the lad and myself. The boy finally dropped down upon the ground before the race ended, having been so convulsed with laughter as to be unable to stand erect, while I only remained standing until the race ended, and then followed my son's example. "Jim" having administered the necessary chastisement to the dog, likewise sought rest on the bosom of mother-earth, while the old cocker, after having sulked a few moments in the woods, came sneakingly out and cautiously approached the contestant in the race, licked affectionately his hand, and then looked up imploringly into his eyes. The dog having thus humbly acknowledged the justice of the punishment which had been inflicted upon him, was then freely forgiven by "Jim," who patted him affectionately on the head and back.

Thus there was perfect harmony between the guide and the spaniel. The dog immediately reclined at "Jim's" side, placed his head affectionately on his master; having assumed a position which enabled him to look wistfully into the latter's face. Our little mongrel dog had not remained entirely inactive during these exciting events. In the race he participated, although falling far behind both actors; nevertheless he barked and wagged his tail continuously, thus showing the joy and interest which he felt in this part of the proceedings, although when the chastisement commenced he drew his tail between his legs, suddenly disappeared in the woods, and only reappeared after the lapse of an hour. This halt by the roadside lasted about three-fourths of an hour and then we started forward once more. We had not proceeded more than half a mile when the spirited barking of the old cocker-spaniel announced that he had found another partridge only a few rods from the road. "Jim" and the boy started off for this game. Five minutes later the report of the lad's gun proclaimed the death of this bird, while the guide and my son soon returned to the highway. They reported that the old dog had made no attempt on this occasion to secure the bird when it fell to the ground, but, on the contrary, he had not moved from where he was standing, and allowed the guide to approach quietly the dead bird and to pocket the same. In fact, it may be here stated that we had no further trouble with this dog during the remainder of the hunt. He had previously shown much affection for "Jim;" but after the race and the chastisement which he received he was certainly doubly affectionate towards his master. He had always hunted faithfully for us, but during the balance of the day he seemed to be more than usually active and found many birds by the roadside.

On one occasion during the afternoon, when he had been absent from us about an hour, we heard him barking sharply a comparatively long distance from the road. His earnest bark satisfied us beyond a doubt that he had found a bird and desired our assistance.

The question was promptly discussed whether we should render the aid which he now sought. The bird was nearly a half-mile from us; would the dog be able to keep the attention of the partridge until one of our party could reach the spot? This seemed rather doubtful, but "Jim" was anxious to make the attempt, while neither myself nor my son desired to offer any objection. He therefore started off with a lively step and very pleasant anticipations. The loud barking of the spaniel continued without any interruption until the death of the bird was announced by the report of "Jim's" fowling-piece. During this time the lad and myself patiently awaited the return of "Jim," but he was absent nearly half an hour, and in the mean time we had rested by the roadside.

The dog returned with his master, and both were apparently well pleased with the result of their labor. The day's sport had been very satisfactory. The boy had killed four birds and "Jim" had bagged two. This result had been accomplished without leaving the road for any considerable period of time, except in the case which has just been reported.  We had now approached within two miles of the village of Maganetawan.  The most of the land bordering on the road had been cleared, was now cultivated, and consequently we did not expect to find any more birds, unless we turned aside from the highway and made search in the woods bordering on the fields.  This course of procedure required a greater effort than we were now inclined to make.  Consequently we continued to plod along the road, and soon arrived at the Maganetawan Hotel, where we were once more kindly met by the proprietor.  It was then about three o'clock in the afternoon, and inasmuch as we were very hungry, having had no dinner that day, our genial host was requested to prepare for us a hot meal.  The order was kindly received and promptly executed, while the charge for this excellent meal for our whole party, consisting of three persons, was only seventy-five cents.

The captain and "Tom" arrived about three hours later, bringing with them our luggage and the trophies of the hunt.  They reported that the wagon which we had engaged to remove our luggage from camp had arrived at the lake-shore on time.  But prior to its arrival the captain had disposed of the venison to the lumbermen in the vicinity, who were engaged in making roads, building shanties, and opening the small outlet of the lake in order that timber cut here during the approaching winter and placed on the ice might be floated away in the spring.  He had likewise taken down the guide's tent, which was standing on the island at the time of our departure, and gathered up the baggage which we had left behind, and moved the same with our canoes to the shore, where it was accessible to the approach of the wagon. Therefore there had been no important delay after the arrival of the team at the lake. The homeward journey was promptly begun, and the tent which we left standing by the roadside in the morning was gathered up by them when they reached this point, after which they proceeded onward to the village of Maganetawan.

The guides remained with us about two hours after their arrival, and assisted us in repacking our baggage after we had exchanged our hunting-suits for those in which we were to travel. It may be here added for the benefit of those readers who are unacquainted in the village of Maganetawan, that it was found impossible to obtain the luxury of a bath-tub, and it was only after a long and diligent search that I found a citizen who was willing to undertake the task of shaving my face, since barbers and barber-shops, are still unknown in this primitive settlement.

Having completed the arrangements for our departure from this village on the following morning at an early hour, we retired to our room for sleep at about ten o'clock in the evening. We were aroused from our slumbers by a hotel servant about three o'clock the next morning; promptly donned our clothing and soon appeared at the foot of the stairs, where we met the man who had called us, and who then informed us that he was in readiness to conduct us to the steamboat which was to convey us to Burk's Falls. He then placed our baggage on an ordinary wheelbarrow, seized the handles, and moved forwards towards the steamboat wharf. This wharf was located about one-half mile from the hotel, and in order to reach it we were compelled to cross the fields, where we encountered many obstacles, especially mud and occasional patches of ice.

The boat, at the moment of our arrival, had already gotten up steam, and moved away from the wharf about fifteen minutes later. She was ably manned by the captain and his jolly crew, which consisted of a single individual, who attended to all the duties required on this steamboat which were not performed by the captain. My son and myself were the only passengers in the cabin of the boat this morning, although she could have carried very comfortably about eight or ten persons.

The village of Burk's Falls is situated on the banks of the Maganetawan River, about thirty-five miles above the village of Maganetawan. The river route by which we were now travelling was very enjoyable, since the scenery is very picturesque. The whole distance is traversed in the short space of five hours under favorable circumstances. My son, after entering the cabin of the steamboat, found his surroundings so favorable to sleep that he promptly entered the embrace of old *Morpheus*, and continued to enjoy the most delightful repose until we had arrived within a few miles of the end of our journeying by water.

Nine o'clock that morning found us seated at Burk's hotel table enjoying a good breakfast, having been promptly transported by an open passenger-wagon to this inn immediately after the arrival of the steamboat. The driver of the wagon patiently waited for us while we breakfasted and then drove us to the railroad depot.

The train on which we were to travel to Toronto did not arrive promptly that morning, and consequently we were compelled to remain at this station about an hour. My son during this period kept a close watch on the market-basket containing the ruffed grouse, which he was very anxious to convey to his mother and sister, who were now stopping at the Queen's Hotel in Toronto, where we expected to arrive about eight o'clock that evening. The train finally arrived, and we promptly entered the cars, which were roughly constructed and primitive in their appearance. There were on the train at the time about twenty passengers. The greater number of them were pioneers from the backwoods, who had that morning left their log cabins for a day's recreation in travel over this newly-constructed railroad, the completion of which was expected to mark a new era of prosperity and happiness in their lives. Among this class of passengers there was one who was especially conspicuous. He was evidently a sturdy son of toil, and had spent several years in the backwoods, although a Scotchman by birth and education, who proclaimed his nativity by his brogue, features, and the dress that he wore.

The appearance of the man indicated that he had already passed threescore years or more. He carried with him on this occasion his bagpipes, and entertained us with his choicest music, while a happy smile lighted up his wrinkled face. He played on the old musical instrument with great energy, and scarcely halted for breath so long as two or three of the passengers seemed willing to give him audience. He manifested much anxiety, whenever the train halted at the different stations along the route, to entertain with his musical performances all the persons in or about the cars. At such times he took great pains to seat himself in such a position that all who heard the music might at the same time behold the instrument and the performer. In this manner the old Scotchman labored the whole forenoon for the entertainment of others, neither asking nor receiving a single penny for his services; but the manner and the expressions of the entertainer indicated that he was even better pleased than those whom he had sought to entertain.

This train dragged along slowly during the forenoon, although there were few stopping-places, since we were passing only through a forest or very sparsely-settled country.

During the afternoon we changed to another train and then proceeded rapidly towards Toronto, where we arrived about half-past eight in the evening. We had anxiously looked forward during the whole day to our arrival at this point, since we earnestly desired to join the other members of our family, who were then stopping at the Queen's Hotel.

The lad returned to his mother and sister greatly elated by his success in hunting, and even to this hour he regards the time thus spent as the happiest period of his life.

That retriever.

# INDEX.

A thunder-storm, 73.
A hard bed, 73.
A shot at a moose, 167.
A youthful driver, 122.
A beaver-house and family, 136.
A hard dinner, bread frozen, 231.
An exciting chase, 144.
An old Scotchman and his bagpipe, 284.
Animal intelligence, 267.
Anton Miltenberger, the photographer, 81.

Baysville, travelling towards, 27.
Baysville, departure from, 28.
Beaver trysting-place, 115.
Bess, Mr., proprietor of the stage line, 97.
Bear's food-supply, 235.
Bear, path of, 225.
Bob Noble, a guide, 69.
Bob Noble in a sad plight, 76.
Boy, killed his first deer, 255.
Boy's first deer-hunt, 253.
Bracebridge reached, 25.
Break camp at Long Lake, 176.
Bride, personal appearance of, 91.
Burk's Falls, departure from, 118.
Burk's Falls, village of, 283.
Buck, manœuvring of, 268.

Camp, break on Long Lake, 175.
Camp near Spence, 105.
Camped on trail leading from Upper Long Lake to Sugar-Bush Lake, 178.
Camped on moose-trail, 196.
Captain Ross " could not kill moose but did kill deer," 204.
Captain Ross angry and disappointed, 206.
Captain Ross made his appearance, 109.
Captain's deer-dogs, 112.
Captain Ross returned to the party, 131.

Captain George Ross, chief guide, 65.
Captain Ross killed the bull moose, 238.
Canadian custom-house officer, 22.
Canoes leaking badly, 28.
Cabin, Harkness's, 241.
Cathedral, St. James', a magnificent structure, 61.
Chase, an exciting, 144.
Chase, moose-, excitement of, 193.
Chase of doe, exciting, 256.
Chase of doe, doubly exciting, 261.
Chief John and his hound, 33.
Chief John and his object, 36.
Chief John, poor, unhappy man, 55.
Chief guide, Captain Ross, 65.
"Chris," our old friend, 99.
Classification of hunters, 3.
Crackers and cheese were obtained, 246.

Departure from Burk's Falls, 118.
Departure from Sphynx Falls, 125.
Departure from Mossup's Landing, 127.
Departure from Lake Rosseau, 102.
Departure from Pickerel Lake, 72.
Departure of the wedding guests, 94.
Departure from Baysville, 28.
Deer-hunt, started on, 49.
Deer, first killed, 52.
Deer-hunt on Long Lake, 141.
Deer- and moose-hunt, preparation for, 80.
Deer-hunt with villagers, 247.
Deer-hunt, the boy's first, 253.
Deer, the first killed by the boy, 255.
Description of the wedding, 88.
Discovery of moose, 210.
Disappointment foreshadowed, 227.
Doe, exciting chase, 256.
Doe, doubly exciting chase, 261.
Dogs are fairly yelling, 263.

# INDEX

Dogs, captain's, deer, 112.
Dr. Pokorney, the old deer-hunter, 43.
Dr. Pokorney's son, 57.
Drying venison, 146.
Drunken orgie of lumbermen, 62.
Dream, photographer's, 163.

Esculapius lost his patience, 28.
Esculapius and Scribe follow John, 38.
Esculapius, a description of, 20.
Esculapius, smiling and happy, 32.
Expert fisherman, the Governor, 35.
Exercise, health-giving power, 13.
Exercise, a remedy for obesity, 8.

Falls, Burk's, departure from, 118.
Falls, Sphynx, departure from, 125.
Fisherman, expert, the Governor, 35.
Fish, Governor off for, 37.
Fishing, Governor and myself went, 65.
"Fire at him!" 212.
Free grant lands, 85.

George set fire to frying-pan, 66.
George Ross, chief guide, 65.
Governor starts for home, 68.
Governor remains silent, 30.
Governor never winced, 32.
Governor an expert fisherman, 35.
Governor off for fish, 37.
Governor arrived in front of cabin, 39.
Governor and Esculapius start for Watte's Creek, 42.
Governor and Esculapius return from Watte's Creek, 46.
Governor and myself went fishing, 65.
Governor, description of, 20.
Goldsmith frightened, 17.
Guides, Indian, habits of, 23.
Guides, employed at Toronto, 24.
Guide, Wellington Ross, 82.

Hard bed, 73.
Hard dinner, bread frozen, 231.
Hard tramp, 245.
Harkness's cabin, 241.
Health-giving power of exercise, 13.
Henry's day with ruffed grouse, 273.

Home, Governor starts for, 63.
Hotel, proprietor of, 16.
Hotel, Pratt's, 63.
Horka-Porka portage, crossing of, 127.
Hunt, deer-, on Long Lake, 141.
Hunters, classification of, 3.
Hunters, how they spend their time, 4.
Hunters, true, 5.
Hunting, benefits derived from, 7.
Hunting, a science and an art, 7.

Indian guides, habits of, 23.
Intelligence of animals, 267.

Jim's revelation, 35.
Jim and the old cocker-spaniel, 275.
Jim goes for the cocker and the cocker is flogged, 277.
John McCarthy, a gamin, 65.
John's inamorata, 37.
John, Chief, object of, 36.
John, Chief, hound of, 33.
John Royall, good services of, 17.

Labor a pleasure, 233.
Lake on mountain-top, 139.
Lake Pickerel, our stay at, 70.
Lake Pickerel, departure from, 72.
Lake Mud, 74.
Lake Loon, camp near, 74.
Lake Sand, start for, 77.
Lake Rosseau, romantic wedding on, 56.
Lake Sugar-Bush, return to, 220.
Lake of Many Islands, 251.
Lake, Hotel, Ten-Mile, 104.
Landing, Mossup's, departure from, 127.
Leaking badly, canoes, 28.
Lean-to, night under, 208.
Long Lake, start for, 137.
Long Lake, deer-hunt, 141.
Lonely night, 240.
Ludicrous scene, 275.
Lumbermen *hors de combat*, 64.
Lumbermen, their drunken orgie, 62.

Maganetawan River, scenery, 114.
Magnificent structure, St. James' Cathedral, 61.

## INDEX.

Miltenberger, the photographer, 81.
Moose and deer, preparation for grand hunt of, 80.
Moose, a shot at, 167.
Moose, trailing, 172.
Moose-calling, 172.
Moose-chase, great excitement of, 193.
Moose-trail, camped on, 196.
Moose-yard, wild excitement in this chase, 198.
Moose, the woods are full of them, 202.
Moose, Captain Ross could not kill, but did kill deer, 204.
Moose, discovery of, 210.
Moose sighted, 212.
Moose bull killed, 214.
Moose cow wounded, 216.
Moose cow wounded and trailed, 217.
Moose-meat, living on, 219.
Moose photographed, 222.
Moose-bull killed by Captain Ross, 238.
Moose reconnoissance, 182.
Moose reconnoissance, delays, etc., 183.
Moose reconnoissance, started on, 185.
Moose reconnoissance, a frugal meal, 189.
Moose reconnoissance, buck killed, 191.
Mountain-top, lake on, 139.
Mossup's Landing, departure from, 127.
Mud Lake, 74.

Noble, Bob, a guide, 69.
Noble, Bob, in a sad plight, 76.

Obesity, exercise a remedy for, 8.
Office, we immediately walked up to, 14.
Our start for home, 282.

Party attacked by fleas, 66.
Partridge which was not killed, 107.
Partridge-shooting, more of this sport, 279.
Physical exertion, effects of, 2.
Photographer Anton Miltenberger, 81.
Photographer in search of partridges, 119.
Photographer wins the prize, 145.
Photographer lost, 152.
Photographer found, 165.
Photographer's wanderings, 156.
Photographer's dream, 163.

Photographer supplied our camp with ruffed grouse, 223.
Photographed moose, 222.
Pickerel Lake, our stay at, 70.
Pickerel Lake, departure from, 72.
Pioneers, their hardships, 84.
Played out, 246.
Poor Goldsmith thoroughly frightened, 17.
Pokorney, Dr., the old deer-hunter, 43.
Pokorney, Dr., son of, 57.
Proprietor of stage-line, Mr. Bess, 97.
Pratt's Hotel, 63.
Proprietor of hotel, 16.

Reconnoissance, moose, 182.
Reconnoissance, moose, delays, etc., 183.
Reconnoissance, moose, started on, 185.
Reconnoissance, moose, a frugal meal, 189.
Reconnoissance, moose, buck killed, 191.
Recreation required, 2.
Restricted, killing of game should be, 134.
Rendezvous, the village, 65.
River Maganetawan, scenery of, 114.
Royall, John, good services of, 17.
Ross, Captain, made his appearance, 109.
Ross, Captain, returned to the party, 131.
Ross, Captain, could not kill moose, but did kill deer, 204.
Ross, Captain, angry and disappointed, 206.
Ross, Captain, chief guide, 65.
Ross, Captain, killed bull moose, 238.
Rosseau, our departure from, 102.
Romantic wedding on an island in Lake Rosseau, 86.

Sand Lake, started for, 77.
Scenery on Maganetawan River, 114.
Scribe prefers a bed of balsam boughs, 31.
Scribe and Esculapius follow John, 38.
Shot at a moose, 167.
Shelbyville, Tenn., 13.
Sighted moose, 212.
Snow-storm, 228.
Son of Dr. Pokorney, 57.
Spence, our camp near, 105.
Sphynx Falls, departure from, 118.
Stay at Pickerel Lake, 70.

## INDEX.

Struce, Mr., our first meeting, 97.
St. James' Cathedral, a magnificent structure, 61.
Storm, rain-, 221.
Storm, thunder-, 73.
Sunday fishing and what followed, 34.
Sugar-Bush Lake, return to, 220.
Surprised wood-chopper, 244.

Ten-Mile Lake Hotel, 104.
The hunt ended, 281.
The old buck, manœuvring of, 268.
The dogs are fairly yelling, 263.
The boy's first deer-hunt, 253.
The boy killed his first deer, 255.
The author and his son, 250.
The ox-team and the old jumper, 242.
The wedding described, 88.
The grand moose- and deer-hunt, preparation for, 80.
The lean-to, night under, 208.
The village rendezvous, 65.
This tramp long to be remembered, 30.
Thunder-storm, 73.
Toronto, guides employed, 24.

Trysting-place, beaver, 115.
Trailing moose, 172.

Unsavory sleeping-apartments, 41.
Unpleasant tramp, 229.

Village rendezvous, 65.
Villagers, deer-hunt with, 247.
Village of Burk's Falls, 283.

Watte's Creek, return of Governor and Esculapius from, 46.
Watte's Creek started for by Governor and Esculapius, 42.
Wedding, romantic, on an island in Lake Rosseau, 86.
Wedding described, 88.
Wedding guests take their departure 94.
Wellington Rose, guide, 82.
What has happened? 264.
Wilderness, unexplored, 12.
Wood-chopper surprised, 244.

Youthful driver, 122.


THE END.

www.ingramcontent.com/pod-product-compliance
Lightning Source LLC
Chambersburg PA
CBHW022117230426
43672CB00008B/1415